CAN-TO-PAN
COOKERY

Ideal for Boaters, Campers, Outdoorsmen, Students, RVers, and Busy Homemakers

by

LYNNE ORLOFF-JONES

Paradise Cay Publications, Inc
Arcata, California

Cover design: Rob Johnson, www.johnsondesign.org
Editing and book design: Linda Morehouse, www.WeBuildBooks.com

Cover image: Photo by Deborah Sherman
Creative Specialist: Victoria Froelicher

Printed in the United States of America
First Edition
ISBN 978-0-939837-83-8

Published by Paradise Cay Publications, Inc.
P. O. Box 29
Arcata, CA 95518-0029
800-736-4509
707-822-9163 Fax
paracay@humboldt1.com

TABLE OF CONTENTS

ACKNOWLEDGMENTS

A huge thanks to all my students and dear friends who cheered me on to keep cooking. Thanks, also, to those who suggested recipe ideas. My travels in Italy, Thailand, Germany, and Mexico provided wonderful insight to foreign cuisines and flavors.

A big toast to Tito Rivano who invited me for numerous dinners aboard his boat when he knew I was too tired to cook.

A special toast with good Shiraz to Glen Taylor, who introduced me to Thai and Indian specialties and Australian wines.

None of this would have happened had my publishers not urged me on . . . thanks, Paradise Cay.

Life is too short not to enjoy good food. Now let's get cooking!

Getting Started

INTRODUCTION

Every cook, from novice to gourmet, appreciates speedy recipes to get food on the table fast. Some folks get stumped if they're missing an ingredient. This is where creativity, improvising, or substituting pays off. Of course, a big smile helps, too. *Can-to-Pan* will shed some light on alternative ways to prepare traditional dishes.

The recipes in this book can easily be prepared on-the-go in boats or RVs, while tent camping, or in dorms with a one-burner hot plate or microwave. A key strategy is to *always* have a well stocked locker. If you want a salad, open a can of green beans, toss it with Italian dressing and a sprinkling of chopped onion and tomato if available, and you're in business.

There are over 1,500 types of canned/packaged foods. Canned foods are fully cooked, so cooking time is heat and eat. A USDA and National Food Processors Association study shows vitamins, minerals, and fiber are the same in canned foods as they are in home-cooked fresh. Specialty foods—sugar-free, salt-free, fat-free, caffeine-free, gluten free, MSG free, and organic—are readily available at most supermarkets. It's amazing what can be found in a bottle, can, or sealed packet.

Can-to-Pan Cookery is designed to brighten your attitude and appease your appetite with tasty, easy-to-prepare meals.

Best wishes to the happy cook.

FREEZE-DRIED FOODS

Freeze-dried foods such as beef stroganoff, shrimp Creole, turkey tetrazzini, vegetables, puddings, cheese sauce, and so forth, only require hot water for reconstitution. Boil water, split open an individual freeze-dried pouch, add water directly into the pouch, and stir a bit. Let the food reconstitute for several minutes, then dig in. The foil pouches are lightweight, compact, and have a long shelf life.

Because freeze-dried products require sophisticated equipment to produce—equipment that removes only water from the food before it is put into a vacuum chamber where all air is pumped out before packaging—they are considered "specialty foods," which is reflected in their price.

AVAILABLE AT

Sports stores that carry backpacker gear (R.E.I., Wilderness Exchange, etc.)

ESSENTIAL GALLEY EQUIPMENT

For cruising sailors or motor homes

Regardless of where you're going or how long you'll be gone, you'll still require the same amount of essential galley equipment. The following gear is more than adequate for any type of vagabond cooking:

1 large fry pan with lid
1 medium fry pan
1 large pot
1 pressure cooker (optional)
coffee or tea pot
large cutting knife
2 large serving spoons
can opener
corkscrew
thermos
steamer basket
grater
potato peeler
collapsible colander
cutting board
potholders
barbecue grill
ice pick
hand soap
dish detergent
scouring powder

cereal bowls
cups
glasses
plates, plastic & paper
silverware
dish pan & drainer
dish cloth
sponge
SOS pads
garbage bags
plastic wrap
aluminum foil
paper towels
matches
mixing bowls
measuring spoons
measuring cups
charcoal briquettes (opt.)
fly swatter
plastic containers

BASIC FOODS FOR STOCKING A GALLEY

Stock your galley with items from each category. Stick with tried and true foods you *know* you like. Add and experiment as you go along. Once you're provisioned properly, you should be able to whip up a meal for any occasion.

None of the Following Requires Refrigeration

SPICES & SEASONINGS	PASTAS AND GRAINS
salt	spaghetti
pepper	noodles
garlic powder	rice (brown, white, wild)
onion powder	macaroni
curry powder	cracked wheat
chili powder	dehydrated hash browns
Italian seasoning	instant mashed potatoes
oregano, basil	instant au'gratin potatoes
cinnamon, nutmeg	potatoes, whole or sliced, canned
Spanish paprika	dried beans: pinto, lima, etc.
Parmesan cheese	Top Ramen noodles
honey, sugar	flour (wheat, white)
vanilla extract	biscuit mix
wasabi (tube or powder)	corn meal
mustard	crackers
ketchup	graham crackers
soy sauce	bread crumbs
Worcestershire sauce	baking powder/baking soda
hot sauce/salsa	Wondra flour/cornstarch
mayonnaise	Stove Top poultry dressing
maple syrup	risotto
vinegar	sweet potato
cooking oil	rice cakes, pita bread, tortillas
lemon juice	cereals (hot or cold)
capers	

SNACKING FOODS	CANNED MEAT, POULTRY
peanuts	roast beef with gravy
popcorn	dried beef
dried fruit	roast beef hash
cheese spreads	corned beef
potato chips	corned beef hash
tortilla chips	ham (nonrefrigerated)
shoestring potatoes	canned chicken breast meat or
peanut butter/jelly	dark chicken
onion soup mix	canned bacon
(for dips)	salami, pepperoni
beef jerky	chile con queso, canned
trail mix	

BASIC FOODS

VEGETARIAN PROTEIN

soy chunks or granules
vegetarian chicken slices (soy)
TVP (Textured Vegetable Protein)
tofu, nonrefrigerated package

CANNED SEAFOOD	CANNED VEGETABLES	
tuna, can or foil pkg.	corn, kernels or cream style	
salmon, can or foil	beans, green, kidney, baked	
smoked salmon pkg.	beans, refried, garbanzo	
shrimp	green peas	
crab meat	tomatoes, whole, stewed, sauce	
oysters	beets	
mackerel	sauerkraut	
clams	mushrooms	carrots
(whole or minced)	asparagus	yams
sardines	palm hearts	Oriental vegetables
anchovies	artichoke hearts	spinach

HEAT & SERVE PREPARED MEALS

Chung King
  Chinese meals
Pizza-in-a-skillet
stir & serve lasagna
prepared Sloppy Joe
beef stew
chili con carne
spaghetti & meatballs
beef tamales
ravioli
enchiladas
macaroni & cheese
Stroganoff dinner
Hamburger Helper
Pad Thai noodles
Indian madras lentils

SOUPS

regular & chunky
Cup-o-Soups, instant
dry soup mixes
broth
bouillon, cubes
  or powdered

BEVERAGES

coffee, regular
  or instant
tea, regular
  or instant
cocoa, packets or box
fruit juice,
  all flavors

CANNED FRUITS

apples
pineapple
peaches
mixed fruits
berry fillings
orange sections
grapefruit
fruit leather/Roll Ups

READY-MADE SAUCES

sweet & sour (powdered or canned)
marinara sauce
pesto
Alfredo
pesto
Mexican/Mole/4 Cheese
teriyaki
Cheddar cheese mix
white & brown gravy
white sauce
Newburg
hollandaise
creamed soups, undiluted
plum sauce/Hoisin/black bean
mango/duck/sweet & sour
red curry sauce
Indian & Thai sauces

PREPARED SALADS

tomato aspic
marinated garden salad
Italian antipasto

Beverages (cont'd)

lemonade powders
sodas
cocktail mixes

DESSERTS & TOPPINGS

pudding
tapioca
fruit cocktail
plum pudding
  & hard sauce
rice pudding
applesauce
packaged cookies
No-Bake pie &
  cake mixes
KrispyTreats
ready-made frosting
chocolate topping,
marshmallow topping,
strawberry, caramel,
butterscotch, hot fudge
  toppings

Prepared Salads (continued)

marinated artichoke hearts
marinated mushrooms
mixed bean salad
marinated herring

MILK PRODUCTS

powdered milk
evaporated milk
  (low fat & regular)
liquid milk in sterilized cartons
powdered buttermilk
soy milk (regular & low fat)
rice milk in cartons
canned goat milk in cartons
chocolate milk in cartons
artificial cream (flavors too)
sweetened condensed milk

STOVES

Be it a one-burner or two-burner stove using propane, butane, alcohol, kerosene, diesel, or natural gas, a stove is a necessity. Wood and charcoal stoves or barbecue grills are alternatives but lack instant flames.

Now That You Have a Stove You Can Easily Improvise an Oven

STOVETOP POTATO BAKER

This two-piece vessel has a flat, double-walled bottom half that sits on the stove burner. Food to be baked should be placed in an ovenproof dish and set on top of the bottom portion. The dome lid is then placed on top. It's the dome lid that creates the baking effect. The heat is regulated by the size of the flame, and I recommend using nothing higher than a medium flame to prevent burning bottoms. There is no precise way to judge cooking temperature, so lift the lid and peek. Stovetop bakers are handy for reheating leftovers or baking potatoes, cobbler, stuffed peppers, or biscuits.

CAMPING TOASTER

This simple device is self-explanatory. You place the toaster on a stove burner and arrange bread slices on top. When one side is golden brown, you flip over bread until the other side is browned.

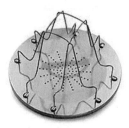

FLAME TAMER

When you place this chromed steel heat diffuser on top of a burner, its double walls ensure even distribution of heat. The flame tamer (also called "heat deflector") creates a double boiler effect that eliminates burned bottoms, scorching, and boiling over. Also, if your oven has a hot spot, you can set the baking dish on top of a flame tamer for more even distribution of heat.

NON-ELECTRIC WAFFLE IRON

This is exactly what the name indicates. It closely resembles
the waffle maker Grandma used on the coal stove. You
pour batter into the iron, lay it directly on top of the stove
burner, cook one side for several minutes, then flip the iron
over and cook the other side. Some waffle irons have gauges
on the outside that indicate degree of doneness—light,
medium, or dark. This ingenious appliance can be found in
specialty or gourmet shops.

PRESSURE COOKER

Many people vividly remember the old-fashioned pressure
cooker that would explode if not properly watched. This
often meant dinner would have to be scraped off the ceiling.
Manufacturers got the idea and installed safety valves to
eliminate such disasters. The most outstanding feature of
a pressure cooker is that you can cook anything in one-
third the normal cooking time and save fuel too. You
can pressure cook anything from stews to whole roasts or
chicken to rice, dried beans, vegetables, or potatoes.

HOW TO BAKE IN A PRESSURE COOKER

Yes, you can bake in a pressure cooker. Put the rack (provided with the cooker) on the bottom of the pressure cooker. Add a half to two-thirds cup of water. Oil a round baking pan that fits snugly in the cooker and put on top of the rack inside the cooker. Pour cake batter (or whatever else you're baking) into the mold, then tightly secure the lid and leave the pressure regulator OFF the vent pipe. Start cooking over a high heat until steam comes out of the vent pipe (about 10 minutes). Reduce heat so only a small flow of steam emerges during the last 20 to 30 minutes. When steam seems to have diminished, the cake should be done. Near the end of baking time, you can remove the lid and check. The pressure cooker is definitely a timesaving and versatile device. (See recipe for pressure cooker bread, page 98.)

SOLAR COOKERS

Solar cookers operate on the principle of light reflecting off a shiny surface, thus creating an intense heat sufficient to cook with. This type of cookery certainly keeps fuel costs down but may present problems on cloudy days. Since solar cooking is so specialized, I recommend using books designed expressly for this method of cooking.

PRESERVING FOODS

The back-to-nature movement stimulated industry to make home preserving appliances. The following methods are too lengthy to discuss here; however, they will give you an idea of various methods:

Drying	Smoking
Pickling	Candying
Corning	Pressure Canning
Canning/Preserving	Salting/Brine

These procedures should be researched before investing time and money. Oftentimes, the process begins with planting seeds and harvesting, following by peeling, slicing, and preserving. If you're not opposed to the work or time involved, the rewards are worthwhile.

CAN-TO-PAN COOKERY

Breakfasts

QUICK-EGGS-A-RONI

1 (8 ounce) package rice & vermicelli mix
or any Rice-A-Roni
1 can cream of chicken soup
6 to 8 eggs

In a large skillet, cook rice according to package directions.
When rice is cooked, stir in undiluted soup. Make 6 hollows in
rice, then drop 1 egg in each hole. Cover with lid and heat till
eggs are set. Sprinkle with Parmesan cheese. Serve immediately.

APPLESAUCE PANCAKE

2 cups pancake mix   2 eggs
1 cup applesauce   1 teaspoon cinnamon

Combine all ingredients and stir till blended. Heat butter
or oil in a skillet; drop batter by spoonfuls into heated oil.
When topside of pancake gets bubbly, flip over and cook
other side. Serve immediately.

FRENCH TOAST

*A wake-up special that will lure even the sleepiest member
out of bed.*

8 to 10 slices bread (cut diagonally, crusts left on)
3 eggs, lightly beaten
¾ cup milk (or powdered milk with water)
½ teaspoon cinnamon
½ teaspoon vanilla
2 teaspoons sugar
dash of nutmeg (optional)

Cut bread and set aside. Mix all other ingredients. Dip bread slices in egg mixture, turning them over so both sides get coated. In a large skillet heat oil, butter. Place bread slices in the hot skillet. Cook on both sides till golden brown. Additional oil may be needed for each batch. Sprinkle with powdered sugar. Serve with maple syrup.

SOUTHERN FRIED POTATOES

An excellent companion for fried eggs. Flour is the secret to a crispy potato.

1 or 2 cans sliced potatoes, drained
½ cup flour or biscuit mix
oil
½ cup chopped onion (optional)
salt and pepper to taste

Lightly dredge the potatoes in flour. Heat about ¼ inch of oil in a skillet. Add potatoes (and onions) and cook till golden brown and crispy on the outside. Sprinkle with salt and pepper. Serve immediately.

EGGS-IN-A-HOLE

Cooking in a moving boat or camper translates into sliding or spilling. To ensure keeping eggs in the skillet, try this simple solution.

1 slice of bread per egg   eggs

Using a glass or cup, cut out a hole in the middle of a slice of bread. (Save bread holes for hors d'oeuvres or bread crumbs.) In a large skillet heat oil and butter, then lay bread slices in pan. Carefully break an egg in the hole. Cook until egg becomes firm, then flip the whole thing over with a spatula and cook other side. Serve immediately.

FRIED EGG SANDWICH

*When you hide bacon and eggs between two pieces of toast,
you may get a little static from your crew. The noise
immediately ceases once they take a bite.*

2 slices of bread (per sandwich)
1 egg (per sandwich)
2 slices cooked bacon (per sandwich)
mayonnaise
garnish with lettuce

Toast the bread. Fry eggs in a skillet, making sure the yolk
is firm. Cook bacon till crisp. Spread mayo on bread, layer
with bacon and egg and lettuce. Top with second slice of
toast. Breakfast is ready.

S.O.S.

*A dish familiar to any serviceman. Remarkably, this is one
dish the mess hall didn't mess up.*

1 onion, chopped
1 teaspoon oil
1 pound ground beef
1 can cream of mushroom soup
½ soup can milk or water
dash of Worcestershire sauce
salt and pepper to taste

In a skillet, sauté onion in oil. Add ground beef and cook
till pink color disappears; drain excess fat. Stir in other
ingredients and simmer for 10 minutes. Serve over toast,
topped with a fried egg.

GERMAN APPLE PANCAKE

PANCAKE
3 eggs
¾ cup milk
¾ cup flour
½ teaspoon salt

FILLING
3 to 4 apples, sliced
¼ cup butter
¼ cup sugar
cinnamon and nutmeg

In a bowl, beat eggs; add milk, flour, and salt. Stir till batter is smooth. Melt butter or oil in a heavy skillet, then pour in batter. Cook with lid on, over a medium heat. While cooking, pancake may produce bubbles, which should be poked down with a fork. When pancake is firm (10 to 15 minutes), remove from heat.

ALTERNATIVE
Place skillet in the oven and bake at 400 degrees for 10 to 15 minutes.

While pancake is cooking, sauté apples in another skillet in ¼ cup of melted butter; add sugar and cinnamon and nutmeg to taste. Cook till tender. After both are cooked, pour apples over pancake and sprinkle with powdered sugar. Cut in wedges and dig in.

OPEN-FACE OMELET

Some gourmet chef, apparently a talented one, began serving omelets in their traditional folded shape. Unfortunately, this delectable dish is somewhat difficult for the average cook to properly flip in half, so consequently people avoid serving it.

My theory is that an omelet is nothing more than scrambled eggs with any combination of filling(s). And quite frankly, I don't think all those splendid ingredients should be buried beneath a layer of egg.

An "open-face omelet" contains ingredients that are almost identical to those found in the formal omelet. The difference is that the open-face omelet is easier to fix. The results, so I've been told, even taste better. Perhaps this is because this dish has more eye appeal and your stomach gets the message quicker.

Besides being delicious and nutritious, this is a clever way to use up small portions of leftover meat, vegetables, or cheese. You almost can't afford not to serve it.

Preparation is always the same regardless of what ingredients you choose. Quantities below serve 4.

EGG MIXTURE
8 eggs (any size)
salt and pepper to taste
spices and herbs (optional)

FILLING(S)
½ cup chopped onion
1 cup any vegetable (cut bite-size)
1 cup leftover meat (optional)
½ cup any grated cheese

STEPS

1. In a bowl beat eggs, milk, salt, and pepper till fluffy, then set aside.
2. In a skillet heat oil or butter. Sauté the onion, then add your choice of vegetables and meat. When using previously cooked leftover meat, just heat till warmed through. Add any additional seasonings.
3. Pour eggs over meat/vegetable mixture. Cook over medium-low heat, stirring to prevent mixture from sticking and to blend ingredients.
    When Using Cheese...
4. Just before eggs become firm, sprinkle with grated cheese. Continue cooking (with or without lid) till it melts. Cut in wedges and serve immediately. Bon appétit!

OMELET COMBINATIONS

ALL TIME FAVORITE
onion
bell pepper
tomato
mushrooms
cheese (optional)

DOG DAY OMELET
onion
bell pepper
hot dogs
cheese (optional)

MEAT COMBO
ham, sausage, bacon,
    beef, Canadian bacon
bell pepper or red pepper
tomato
cheese (optional)

HAVE-A-HEART OMELET
artichoke hearts
onion
bell pepper or red pepper

TOUCH O' ITALY OMELET
ground beef or Italian
    sausage
bell pepper
tomato
mushroom
onion
cheese
(optional) pour heated
    Italian sauce over omelet

FAR-OUT EASTERN SPANISH OMELET
bean sprouts   onion
bamboo shoots   chorizo
shrimp   bell pepper or hot pepper

Season with dash of soy sauce. Pour heated Mexican salsa
over omelet before serving.

CHEESE OF ASPARAGUS OMELET
asparagus
cheese (2 types), Cheddar & Monterey jack

OTHER SUGGESTIONS

VEGETABLES	MEATS (ANY LEFTOVERS)
celery	salami
zucchini	corned beef
carrots	steak
avocado	chicken/turkey
spinach	smoked salmon
eggplant	& cream cheese

SOUPER POACHED EGGS

1 can Cheddar cheese soup (or cream of celery)
½ cup milk
6 eggs
3 English muffins, split and toasted
or 6 slices toast

In a skillet blend soup and milk; heat to boiling. Gently
break eggs into soup sauce; cook over low heat until eggs are
firm. Place eggs on toasted English muffins or toast slices
and pour soup sauce over eggs.

FRIED APPLES & OATS

2 medium apples, chopped
3 tablespoons butter
1½ cups rolled oats, uncooked*
1 egg, beaten
½ cup water
4 tablespoons brown sugar
1 teaspoon cinnamon

Sauté apples in butter. In a separate bowl, combine oats and the egg until the oats are coated. Add the oats mixture to the apples and cook over medium heat for 3 to 5 minutes, stirring constantly until the oats are dry, separated, and lightly browned. Add remaining ingredients; continue cooking for 2 to 3 minutes until the liquid evaporates. Serve as breakfast or brunch.

*If using instant oats, increase the water to ¾ cup and decrease brown sugar by 1 tablespoon.

HASH 'N EGGS

1 large can corned beef hash
4 eggs
½ cup grated cheese
1 (2 ounce) can diced chile peppers (optional)

Place hash in a large, well greased skilled. Make four shallow depressions, one for each egg. Break an egg into each depression and sprinkle with cheese and chiles. Place lid on pan and cook over a low heat until the eggs are done to your liking.

HUEVOS RANCHEROS

1 jar (8 ounce) Mexican salsa
4 eggs
1 cup grated cheese
tortillas

In a large skillet bring salsa to a low boil. Break eggs into
salsa. Cover, and lower heat. Cook until the eggs are
almost done, then sprinkle cheese and continue cooking
until it has melted. Place a tortilla on a plate and spoon on
eggs, cheese, and salsa. Use additional tortillas as a scoop.

HEARTY BREAKFAST CASSEROLE

2 cans sliced potatoes, drained
1½ tablespoons oil
salt and pepper to taste
½ cup chopped onion
½ cup chopped bell pepper
1 cup leftover meat
4 eggs
½ cup shredded cheese

In a large skillet, sauté half the potatoes in oil; sprinkle with
salt and pepper. Top with a layer of half the onions and bell
pepper. Arrange half the meat on top.
REPEAT THE LAYERS
Cover and cook over low heat for 10 minutes. In a bowl,
beat the eggs, then pour over vegetable/meat mixture.
Continue cooking until eggs are firm (about 7 minutes).
Top with cheese; cover until cheese melts (about 2 minutes).
Cut in wedges and serve.

JOHNNY CAKE

A quick breakfast bread everyone will enjoy.

½ cup butter
⅓ cup sugar
2 eggs
1¾ cup buttermilk
1 cup cornmeal
1 cup flour
2 teaspoons baking powder
¾ teaspoon salt
¾ teaspoon baking soda

Cream butter and sugar. Beat in eggs, then add buttermilk. In a separate bowl, mix all dry ingredients, then add to the creamed mixture. Grease and lightly flour a baking pan and pour in mixture. Bake at 375 degrees for 30 to 40 minutes Serve with plenty of butter and jam.

MUESLI

(Copycat ready-to-eat cereal served in Great Britain)

Mix the following ingredients in a big bowl and store in an airtight container.

4 cups uncooked oats (instant or regular)
½ cup wheat germ
½ cup unsalted (shelled) sunflower seeds
½ cup hazelnuts
½ cup raisins
¼ cup unprocessed bran (optional)
¼ to ½ cup any dried fruit (prunes, dates, etc.), optional

Scoop out a handful of cereal, put in a bowl, add milk, and eat.

Lunches

SHRIMP KEBABS

1 pound large shrimp, rinsed (leave shells on)
1 to 2 bananas, cut into chunks
cherry tomatoes, whole (about a cup)
1 bunch green onions, cut in half
1 red or yellow pepper, cut into chunks

MARINADE
½ cup oil   ¼ cup vinegar
salt   garlic powder
pepper   Italian seasonings
                     dried chili pepper flakes

Prepare marinade. Marinate the raw shrimp for at least 30
minutes. Then thread a skewer, alternating shrimp with
vegetables. Barbecue 5 to 7 minutes, turning once. Brush
kebabs with marinade while grilling. When shrimp are pink,
they're done.

BROCCOLI SALAD

1 bunch broccoli florets, cooked to crunchy
(or microwave broccoli for 3 minutes)
3 tablespoons seasoned rice vinegar
1 tablespoon soy sauce
3 tablespoons water
1 tablespoon sesame seeds

While broccoli is cooking, mix remaining ingredients in a
bowl. Add cooked broccoli, then cover the bowl with a lid
and shake until all pieces of broccoli are covered with liquid.
Can be eaten after a short marinade time, but tastes better
when marinated a few hours.

GRILLED VEGETABLES

2 teaspoons oil
1 cup eggplant, sliced thin vertically
1 cup tomatoes, sliced
1 cup yellow squash, sliced thin vertically
1 onion, sliced thin
1 potato, sliced thin
2-3 cloves garlic, minced
generous sprinkles of salt, pepper, any assortment of
herbs & spices

Spread oil on a large square of aluminum foil. Spread the
vegetables on the foil, sprinkle with seasoning, and drizzle
with oil. Securely crimp edges. Place on barbecue grill and
cook for about 10–15 minutes, turning occasionally.

BBQ SKIRT STEAK FOR FAJITAS

2 pounds skirt steak, trimmed of excess fat

MARINADE
½ cup lemon juice
4 cloves minced garlic
1 teaspoon each oregano and cumin, salt and pepper
splash of oil

Prepare marinade. Marinate meat for several hours. Lay
meat on the grill and cook about 6 minutes for rare. Baste if
you wish. When done, thinly slice meat across the grain.

SERVE WITH: Warmed flour tortillas, salsa, and beans.
Guacamole and sour cream are more options for toppings.

GRILLED FRUIT

2 teaspoons oil
½ cube butter
sliced nectarines, peaches, banana, pineapple, apple
(any combo)
3 tablespoons brown sugar
1 teaspoon cinnamon, nutmeg
biscotti or cookie crumbs (optional)

Spread oil and a little butter on a square of aluminum foil.
Spread fruit on the foil, and top with butter pats, sugar,
and seasonings. Securely crimp the foil edges. Place on
barbecue grill and cook for about 5 minutes, turning a time
or two. Open and sprinkle with crumbs. Serve.

TAILGATE TORTILLA

1 large ripe avocado
1 minced garlic clove
salt and pepper to taste
4 flour tortillas
1 cup cooked shredded chicken (or 1 can chicken meat)
3 slices bacon, cooked and crumbled (optional)
1 cup grated Monterey cheese
Garnishes: shredded lettuce or chili peppers

Mash the avocado and blend in other ingredients. Set aside.
Spread the avocado mixture on the flour tortillas. Then
spread the chicken, bacon, cheese, and other garnishes. Roll
up and serve.

HOT CHEESE SAUCE SANDWICHES

4 English muffins, split and toasted
sliced ham or Canadian bacon
1 large tomato, sliced
Baco-bits

Heat muffins, then layer with ham or Canadian bacon and tomato slices sprinkled with Baco-bits. Spoon hot "almond cheese sauce" over and serve.

ALMOND CHEESE SAUCE

¼ cup butter	1 jar (5 ounce) processed American
3 tablespoons flour	cheese sauce
¼ teaspoon salt	1 tablespoon sherry or white wine
1¼ cup milk	⅓ cup slivered almonds

Melt butter in saucepan, then blend in flour and salt. When bubbly, stir in milk until thickened. Then stir in cheese spread and stir until melted. Mix in sherry and almonds and heat for a few minutes.

HASH BURRITOS

1 large can corned beef or roast beef hash
1 (4 ounce) can diced chiles
grated Cheddar cheese
flour or corn tortillas (warmed)

In a large skillet heat hash, chiles. Fill tortillas with mixture and sprinkle on cheese. Roll up and wrap burrito style.

POLYNESIAN CHICKEN SALAD

1 cup mayonnaise
½ cup chutney
½ teaspoon each salt and pepper
3 cups cooked chicken or fish (canned or fresh)
1 (8 ounce) can pineapple tidbits, drained
1 can sliced water chestnuts, drained
½ cup chopped Macadamia nuts

In a bowl mix together mayonnaise, chutney, salt, and pepper. In a separate bowl combine chicken, pineapple, water chestnuts, and chopped nuts. To serve, spoon mayonnaise mixture over chicken mixture. Sprinkle with toasted coconut. Instead of presenting in dishes, serve in scooped-out cantaloupe shells.

PEPPERONI & BEAN DIP-WICH

4 slices bread, toasted
½ cup commercial canned bean dip
sliced pepperoni or salami
onion slices, paper-thin
bell pepper rings

Spread bean dip on toasted bread slices. Top with pepperoni, onion, and pepper rings.

EGG & MEAT-WICH

3 hard-cooked eggs
2 teaspoons chopped pickle (optional)
ham slices
2 tablespoons mayonnaise
onions sliced paper-thin
salt and pepper to taste

Chop eggs and combine with mayonnaise, salt, pepper, and pickle. Spread mustard lightly on bread; top with egg mixture, meat, and onion slices.

NOTE: For a unique flavor combine ¼ cup mayonnaise with ½ teaspoon ground ginger. Use in place of plain mayonnaise.

TUNA & PINEAPPLE SANDWICH

1 can tuna, drained
½ cup crushed pineapple, drained
salt & pepper to taste
½ cup each diced celery and bell or red pepper
½ teaspoon ginger powder

Mix all ingredients and spread on bread. Slice diagonally and serve.

SARDINE SANDWICH

1 can sardines, drained
1 hard-cooked egg, sliced
1 onion sliced thin
1 tablespoon each mayonnaise and mustard

Spread mayonnaise/mustard mixture on bread. Arrange sardines, egg, and onion slices between halves.

SALMON-CUCUMBER SANDWICH

1 can salmon
¼ cup onion, chopped
¼ cup celery, chopped
½ cup mayonnaise
1 tablespoon parsley (optional)
salt and pepper to taste
bread slices

Drain and flake salmon; add other ingredients except
cucumber mix. Spread salmon mixture on bread and top
with marinated cucumber slices.

MARINATED CUCUMBERS
In a small bowl combine 1 cucumber, sliced thinly, with ½
cup vinegar, 1 teaspoon sugar, and ¼ teaspoon salt. Cover
and chill for 1 to 2 hours till flavors blend.

CURRIED TUNA SANDWICH

1 can tuna, drained and flaked
1 teaspoon curry powder
¼ cup chopped black olives
salt and pepper to taste
¼ cup mayonnaise, or plain yogurt
1 tablespoon minced bell pepper
tomatoes diced (optional)

Combine all ingredients and mix well. Spread tuna mixture
on bread and slice diagonally.

CHICKEN & BEAN SPROUT SANDWICH

1 can bean sprouts, drained OR 1 cup fresh sprouts
1 tablespoon diced onion
2 tablespoons chopped radishes
1 teaspoon soy sauce
2 tablespoons mayonnaise
bread slices
1 cup cooked chicken, shredded
salt, garlic powder, and ginger powder to taste

Combine sprouts, onion, radishes, and soy sauce and let
stand for 30 minutes to blend flavors. Spread mayonnaise
on bread. Arrange chicken on top of bread slices and
sprinkle with salt and seasonings. Top with sprout mixture.

MOCK REUBEN SANDWICH

Thousand Island dressing or mustard & mayo mixture
8 slices rye bread
1 can corned beef
1 can sauerkraut, well drained
1 slice Swiss cheese per sandwich

Spread mustard and mayonnaise on bread. Layer corned
beef, sauerkraut, and cheese. Close sandwich. Melt oil in
skillet and brown sandwich until the cheese melts.

HOT VEGETABLE SANDWICH

1 onion, chopped
½ bell or red pepper, chopped
1 tablespoon oil
any combo chopped vegetables:
    zucchini, broccoli, tomatoes, asparagus, cabbage
salt and pepper
1 teaspoon each Italian seasoning and garlic powder
¼ cup Parmesan cheese
crunchy rolls, heated

Sauté onion and bell pepper in 1 tablespoon oil. Add
chopped vegetables; heat until tender. Add all other
ingredients; heat and stir. Sprinkle with Parmesan cheese.
Serve on crunchy heated rolls.

SOUP SANDWICHES

1 can chunky sirloin burger soup
1 can French fried onion rings
½ cup shredded cheese (preferably Cheddar)
bread or buns
tomato slices and lettuce garnish

In saucepan combine all ingredients. Heat until cheese melts.
Serve on bread or buns. Garnish with tomato and lettuce.

TUNA CAKES

1 can kidney beans, drained
1 egg, beaten
1 can tuna, drained and flaked
½ cup onion
⅓ cup parsley (optional)
1 teaspoon lemon juice
salt and pepper to taste
bread crumbs for coating

Mash beans with a fork, then add beaten egg. Mix in other ingredients, except bread crumbs. Using about ⅓ cup of tuna mixture, shape into patties, then roll in breead crumbs. Fry patties in hot oil, turning to brown both sides. Serve immediately.

CHICKEN OR TUNA OR SHRIMP SALAD SANDWICHES

1 can of chicken OR a can of the following:
    ham, or shrimp, or tuna
¼ cup of each: celery and onion
½ cup mayonnaise (more or less to suit taste)
½ teaspoon prepared mustard
1 hard-cooked egg, crumbled
1 tablespoon minced pickle, optional
salt and pepper to taste

Combine all ingredients. Serve as a sandwich or stuffed in a tomato.

CHEESE & PIMIENTO SANDWICH

1 cup shredded cheese
¼ cup mayonnaise
¼ cup chopped onion or celery
¼ teaspoon Worcestershire sauce
salt and pepper to taste
1 jar pimientos
1 teaspoon mustard (preferably spicy)
tomato slices
pickle

Mix together first 7 ingredients. Spread mixture on good whole grain bread. Garnish with tomato slices and pickle.

SHRIMP FOO YUNG

4 eggs, beaten
2 cups bean sprouts
2 green onions, chopped

SAUCE
½ teaspoon sugar
1 tablespoon soy sauce

1 (8-ounce) can shrimp
1 can shrimp, drained
⅛ teaspoon each: salt,
    pepper, garlic powder

¼ cup chicken broth
(optional) thicken with
1 teaspoon cornstarch

In a bowl combine eggs, bean sprouts, onion, shrimp, and
seasonings. In a skillet heat the oil. Add ¼ cup mixture for
each patty. Fry the patties until lightly set and browned. Set
aside on a platter. Prepare sauce: combine sugar, soy sauce,
and chicken broth, heat over low heat for a few minutes;
if desired, thicken with cornstarch, stirring well to avoid
lumps. Drizzle sauce over patties.

ORIENTAL PANCAKES

8 pancakes (follow package instructions)
¾ cup each: (diced) celery, onion, bell pepper
1 teaspoon oil
OR
1 can oriental vegetables, drained, in place of celery/onion
¾ cup mayonnaise
1 tablespoon mustard
¾ cup milk
1 can tuna, drained
salt, pepper, & soy sauce to taste
1 can chow mein noodles

Prepare 8 pancakes following package instructions. Set
aside and keep warm. Sauté celery, onion, and bell

pepper in oil, or heat the canned vegetables. In a bowl mix mayonnaise, mustard, and milk; stir in tuna, salt, pepper, soy sauce, and chow mein noodles. Add mixture to vegetables in the skillet and stir till heated through. Spread a layer of mixture on top of pancake, top with another pancake (like a sandwich). Top "sandwich" with a spoonful of mixture and serve immediately.

WELSH RABBIT

A basic dish to satisfy a cheese craving.

1 tablespoon butter
2 cups grated Cheddar cheese
½ cup beer (stale is OK)
¼ teaspoon dry mustard
¼ teaspoon hot sauce
toasted bread or English muffins
garnish with bacon strip, tomato slice

Melt butter in double boiler. Add cheese and stir continuously until it begins to melt. Pour in beer, dry mustard, and hot sauce. Stir until smooth. Pour over hot toast; top with any of the garnishes. Thicken with flour if mixture is too thin.

GRINGO-STYLE TACOS

Here's a zesty way to improvise a taco.

1 tablespoon oil
½ onion, diced
1 bell pepper, chopped (optional)
1 can roast beef with gravy OR 1 pound cooked ground beef
1 package taco seasoning

TACO TOPPINGS
1 cup shredded lettuce   2 tomatoes, chopped
taco sauce (jar or bottle)   ½ cup any grated cheese
chopped avocado

In a skillet with 1 tablespoon oil, sauté the onion and bell
pepper. Add meat, then sprinkle in taco seasoning and
water. Blend ingredients and simmer until heated through.
Spoon about ¼ cup of the meat mixture into each taco shell.
Garnish with any of the toppings.

OPEN-FACE PIZZAWICH

*This Italian flavored wonder is a lifesaver when you're in
doubt what to serve for a fast snack. To serve 4:*

bread, tortilla or pita bread
½ bell or red pepper, chopped
½ onion, chopped
artichoke hearts, pepperoni tomato, pineapple (options)
½ cup mozzarella or Monterey, grated or sliced thin
1 small can tomato sauce, cheese, or pizza sauce
Parmesan cheese for topping
generous sprinkles of: salt, pepper, garlic powder, Italian
    seasoning

Toast bread, then arrange slices on cookie sheet or aluminum foil. Spread a thick layer of tomato sauce on toast, then sprinkle with spices. Next, spread about 2 tablespoons of each vegetable. Sprinkle the grated cheese evenly over the toast slice. Place under hot broiler for about 2 minutes or until cheese melts. Sprinkle with Parmesan cheese. Serve immediately.

VEGETARIAN BURRITO

1 tablespoon oil	1 can mild chiles, drained
1 onion, chopped	salt, pepper, chili powder
1 8-ounce jar enchilada sauce	flour tortillas
1 can refried beans	½ cup cheese, shredded

Heat 1 tablespoon oil in a skillet, then sauté the onion until tender. Add half the enchilada sauce, beans, chiles, and spices. Simmer for 10 minutes. Spoon about 3 tablespoons of bean mixture in the center of each tortilla. Roll up tortillas and arrange in baking dish. Sprinkle on cheese and pour on remaining enchilada sauce. Bake at 350 degrees for 20 minutes. Serve hot from the oven.

AVOCADO SANDWICH

1 ripe avocado
1 tablespoon chopped onion
dash of hot sauce
salt, pepper, and garlic powder to taste
garnishes: shredded lettuce, chopped tomatoes, cilantro

With a fork, mash avocado; add other ingredients and blend well. Spread on bread or roll up in a flour tortilla. Top with garnishes.

MEAT THE BEET SANDWICH

¼ cup mayonnaise
1 teaspoon horseradish
sandwich meat, sliced (turkey, ham)
1 small can sliced beets, drained
1 onion, sliced thin
lettuce or sprouts, optional

Combine mayonnaise and horseradish and spread on bread.
Arrange meat, and top with slices of beets and onion and lettuce.

CREPES

*Manufacturers have flooded the market with specialty items
such as crepe makers, prepared crepe mix, and frozen crepes.
These conveniences are handy, but all that's really needed
to turn out a perfect crepe is flour, milk, eggs, butter, and an
ordinary skillet. Crepes are a versatile dish—use as a main
dish, dessert, or for a snack.*

BASIC CREPE RECIPE
⅓ cup flour
1¼ teaspoon salt
2 eggs
1 cup milk
1 tablespoon melted butter

Beat eggs in bowl. Add flour, butter, and milk; blend until
batter is smooth. In a small skillet, pour a scant ¼ cup
batter. Cook for 1½ minutes until top is set; the underside
will be slightly browned. Loosen crepe and cook other side
for about 30 seconds. Slip cooked crepe into plate; keep
warm while you cook other crepes. Yields about 10 crepes.

FILLED CREPES

Spoon a heaping tablespoon or two of filling across the center of the lighter side of crepe. Roll up and place side by side on plate. If they are to be heated, place in a baking dish.

UNFILLED CREPES

Spoon filling on top of crepe and arrange on platter. If topping (such as cheese) requires melting, arrange on cookie sheet and briefly place under broiler.

DESSERT CREPE

Use Basic Crepe Recipe, but add 2 tablespoons sugar. (Optional: 2 tablespoons brandy or rum.) Add ice cream or sherbet, topped with whipped cream or topped with either applesauce & cinnamon or hot fudge sauce & strawberries.

SNACKS CREPE

Spread crepe with meat and cheese, roll, and serve chilled. Wrap one of the following fillings in crepe and fry in oil till brown:

cooked sliced sausage
sweet & sour pork
cheese cubes
cottage cheese with blueberries

BEANS & RICE

A tasty way to use leftover rice.

1 onion, chopped
1 tablespoon oil
1 small can diced chile peppers
2 cans kidney beans, drained
1 teaspoon garlic powder
1 teaspoon cumin or Mexican seasoning
2 tomatoes, chopped
3 cups hot cooked rice

Sauté onion in 1 tablespoon oil. Add remaining ingredients except rice. Stir over low heat for 10 minutes—beans may become semi-mashed. Serve over rice, or roll into a heated corn tortilla.

THREE BEAN CHILI

1 pound ground turkey or ground beef
1 large onion, diced
1 can tomato sauce
1 can chopped tomatoes (don't drain)
1 can kidney beans
1 can pinto beans
1 can black beans
1 packet chili con carne seasoning
OR
use your own spices
1 teaspoon salt, pepper, chili powder, garlic powder, cumin powder, cayenne papper*   *use sparingly

In a large skillet cook the meat and onion. Drain excess fat. Add all other ingredients. Simmer until thoroughly heated. Ummmm good!

MOCK BOUILLABAISSE SOUP

The only thing "mock" about this recipe is the substitution of canned fish for fresh.

1 can tomato soup
1 can chicken gumbo soup or chicken broth
2 soup cans water
1 (16 ounce) can tomatoes
½ cup bell pepper, chopped
½ cup celery, chopped
½ onion, chopped
1 tablespoon parsley
1 tablespoon Worcestershire sauce
½ teaspoon garlic powder or
1 clove garlic minced
1 bay leaf
1 (4½ ounce) can shrimp, drained
1 (8 ounce) can minced clams, undrained
salt and pepper to taste

Combine soups, water, tomatoes, bell pepper, celery, onion, parsley, Worcestershire, garlic, and bay leaf. Bring to boil, then reduce heat and simmer till vegetables are tender. Add shrimp and undrained clams and simmer until heated through. Season with salt and pepper to taste. Remove bay leaf. Makes 6 to 8 servings. Serve with hot French bread.

HELPFUL HINTS

BAKING/COOKING

1. To avoid measuring flour or sugar, pour a premeasured cup into your hand to get an idea of how much fills your cupped hand.
2. For lighter, fluffier pancakes or waffles, use club soda instead of milk.
3. Improvise a colander by punching holes in an aluminum foil pan.
4. Before measuring honey, syrup, or molasses, spray the cup with a nonstick spray.
5. Rather than dirty a bowl for mixing cake batter, use the backpackers' trick and "moosh" all ingredients in a sealed ziploc bag. When ingredients are blended, unzip and pour into a baking pan.
6. Marinate meats in ziploc bags and avoid another clean-up.
7. When dividing a recipe in half, use this rule of thumb for eggs: Lightly beat the egg. 1½ teaspoons equals one-half an egg, 1 teaspoon equals ⅓ egg.
8. Use a strand of uncooked spaghetti to test doneness of a deep cake. (Sometimes toothpicks are too short.)
9. Shape ground beef into patties before freezing. Shape with wet hands for an extra fast and neat job. Separate patties with waxed paper. Frozen patties barbecue just fine.
10. A stale egg will float or tilt to the top of a bowlful of water. Throw out floaters. Fresh eggs should sink to the bottom.

(For the entire list of helpful hints, see Appendix, p. 142.)

Dinners

HOMEMADE PIZZA
(NO-RISE DOUGH METHOD)

Pizza has become as American as apple pie. This simplified dough method eliminates waiting for yeast dough to rise.

DOUGH
2 cups biscuit mix
½ cup water

Mix the biscuit mix and water together. Knead for about 1 minute. Roll the dough on a floured board till it fits a pizza pan or cookie sheet. Pinch edges to form crust.

TOPPING
1 pound ground beef or Italian sausage, cooked & crumbled
8 ounces mozzarella cheese, grated
1 can pizza sauce (spaghetti or tomato sauce will do)
2 teaspoons garlic powder (or fresh garlic, minced)
½ teaspoon salt and pepper
1 teaspoon Italian seasoning
½ teaspoon oregano

ADDITIONAL TOPPINGS (OPTIONAL)
onions, bell or red pepper, anchovies, pepperoni, black olives, salami

PROCEDURES TO ASSEMBLE PIZZA
The secret of this pizza is the order in which it's put together. It's *very important* not to vary these steps. Regardless of which ingredients you choose, the sequence of building must remain the same.
Step 1: Cheese—working from the bottom up, firmly press cheese into dough.
Step 2: Meat and any other ingredient—generously cover the pizza as evenly as possible with these ingredients.
Step 3: Spices—sprinkle spices over the pizza.
Step 4: Pizza sauce—always on the top, spread sauce over pizza.

Optional: Sprinkle extra cheese on top for eye appeal.
Bake in preheated oven for 20 to 25 minutes at 425 degrees.
Serve piping hot.

CAJUN JAMBALAYA

1 teaspoon oil	1½ cup instant white rice
1 onion cut into chunks	1 can stewed tomatoes
1 bell pepper, cut bite-size	1 cup water
1 clove garlic, minced	salt and pepper to taste
½ pound kielbasa cut bite-size	hot sauce or Cajun season-ing to taste

In a large skillet, heat 1 teaspoon oil and sauté the onion,
bell pepper, and garlic. Add the kielbasa. Then add the rice,
tomatoes, water and seasoning. Cover and cook 7 minutes,
until rice has absorbed the liquid. Serve immediately.

CAMPERS BEEF STEW BOURGUIGNONNE

When all fresh food is gone you can still eat hearty.

1 large can beef stew
2 cans French fried onion rings
dash of Worcestershire sauce
¼ teaspoon each salt, pepper, garlic powder, thyme
1 can mushrooms, drained
½ cup red wine
1 cup any vegetable, optional
1 can carrots sliced, or fresh sliced carrots

Mix all ingredients in a pot and heat over a medium
flame. If you like a thicker stew, thicken with non-lumping
Wondra Flour.

HAM & YAM & APPLES

1 pound canned ham
1 can yam, drained and sliced
2 apples, sliced
2 tablespoons brown sugar
2 to 4 tablespoons orange juice if available (OK to omit)

Brown ham on both sides in a large skillet or dutch oven.
Arrange yams and apples around ham. Sprinkle with
brown sugar and orange juice. Cover and cook on low heat
till apples are tender and ham and yams are heated. Baste
with pan juices, adding water if ham sticks to bottom of
pan.

MEATBALL STEW

1 onion, chopped
3 cups frozen meatballs
1 can tomatoes, chopped
1 can any vegetable
1 can green beans, drained
1 teaspoon Worcestershire sauce
2 tablespoons parsley flakes
1 teaspoon each basil & garlic powder

Sauté onion in a large skillet. Add remaining ingredients,
including tomato liquid. Simmer for 20 minutes. Serve
over rice or noodles

HOT DOG & KRAUT DINNER

1 small onion, diced
2 teaspoons oil
6 hot dogs, cut bite size
1 can sauerkraut, drained
½ teaspoon caraway seed (optional)
1 can sliced potatoes
1 apple, sliced
salt and pepper to taste
mustard

Sauté onion in skillet with 2 teaspoons oil. Add remaining
ingredients and heat through, stirring occasionally. Serve
with mustard.

MASHED POTATO MEAT PIE

½ cup cornflake crumbs
4 cups mashed potatoes (follow package directions)
2–3 tablespoons butter
3 eggs
½ cup diced Mozzarella cheese
½ cup Parmesan cheese, grated
½ cup cooked meat, cut bite-size
salt and pepper to taste
paprika for garnish

Grease a pie pan, then sprinkle with half the cornflake
crumbs. Add butter to the mashed potatoes, then add eggs,
cheeses, salt and pepper, and beat until fluffy. Stir in the
meat. Spoon mashed potato mixture into pie pan. Sprinkle
with remaining crumbs and dust with paprika for pretty
coloring. Bake 30 minutes at 350 degrees, or until puffed and
golden brown.

SALAMI STEW

Salami is too versatile to be restricted to sandwiches.

1 cup salami, cut bite-size
1 cans chunky minestrone soup
½ teaspoon each Italian seasoning and garlic powder
1 cup garbanzo beans
½ onion, diced (optional)

Add all the ingredients and stir until heated through. Serve with French bread.

GROUND BEEF STEW

1 pound ground beef
½ cup water
1 envelope onion soup mix
salt, pepper, garlic powder to taste
1 can tomatoes (or stewed tomatoes), drained
1 can vegetables (or 1 cup any fresh vegetable)

In a skillet brown ground beef; drain excess fat. Stir in other ingredients and simmer for 20 minutes. Serve over rice or noodles.

BROWN BREAD & BAKED BEANS

Filling enough for a dinner meal.

1 large can S&W baked beans
1 large can S&W brown bread
butter for bread

Warm the beans in a pot or pan, making sure they don't
stick to bottom. While beans are heating, warm the brown
bread by either steaming or baking it. Serve when both are
heated through.

NOTE: For a heartier version, sauté a small can of Spam,
chopped in bite-size pieces, then add to beans.

VEGETARIAN SPAGHETTI

⅓ cup olive oil
½ cup chopped onion
6 cloves minced garlic
½ cup chopped red or bell pepper
1 large can Italian tomatoes
8 ounces spaghetti (cooked following package directions)
salt and pepper to taste
pinch of sugar
splash of red wine (optional)
Parmesan cheese

In a skillet, sauté the onion, garlic, and peppers in olive
oil till tender. Stir in the canned tomatoes. If you prefer a
thicker sauce, then add one small can tomato paste. Add
seasonings and stir. Simmer for 10–15 minutes. Serve over
hot pasta with generous sprinkle of Parmesan cheese.

CAMP STYLE SAUERBRATEN

1 (12 ounce) can roast beef
   with gravy
⅓ cup canned mincemeat
½ cup beef bouillon

1 tablespoon brown sugar
1 tablespoon vinegar
½ teaspoon ground ginger
cornstarch to thicken

Put all ingredients in a large skillet, and stir to break up any chunks. Cook until heated through. If necessary, thicken with cornstarch dissolved in ¼ cup hot water. Serve with hot potato pancakes or noodles.

CHICKEN & HAM STEW

1 onion chopped
1 cup ham, cut bite-size
1 can white meat chicken
1½ teaspoons oil

1 can sliced potatoes, drained
1 can mixed veggies, drained
½ cup chicken broth
bulgur wheat, cooked

Sauté onion, ham and chicken in 1½ teaspoons oil. Add other ingredients and simmer for 12 minutes or until heated through. Accompany with cooked bulgur wheat.

FRIED RICE

1 onion, chopped
1 bell pepper, chopped
2 tablespoons oil
1 to 2 cups leftover ham or
chicken (cut bite-size)
4 cups cooked rice (according to package directions)
2 to 3 teaspoons soy sauce
2 eggs, lightly beaten
salt and pepper to taste

In a skillet, sauté onion and bell pepper in 2 tablespoons oil;
cook until barely tender. Add meat and stir for 2 minutes.
Blend in the rice and soy sauce. Add eggs and continue
stirring the mixture until eggs are firm. Heat for 5 more
minutes. Serve immediately.

MACARONI & HAM CASSEROLE

1 onion, chopped
1 bell pepper, diced
2 cups ham cut bite-size
2 teaspoons oil

2 cans macaroni & cheese
1 can tomatoes, drained
dash of Worcestershire

In a skillet sauté onion, bell pepper, and ham in 2 teaspoons
oil. Blend in macaroni and cheese and tomatoes. Season
with Worcestershire sauce. Simmer for 10 minutes. Serve
immediately.

SPEEDY STROGANOFF

1 can mushrooms, drained
1 onion, chopped
1 teaspoon oil
1 can roast beef with gravy

½ cup sour cream
dash of Worcestershire
1 teaspoon garlic powder
rice or noodles, cooked

Sauté mushrooms and onion in a teaspoon of oil. Add canned roast beef, sour cream, and seasonings. Stir occasionally until mixture is heated. Serve over rice or noodles.

CREAMY CHIPPED BEEF

Chipped beef is usually served with white sauce; however, here's a zesty alternative for a basic dish.

boiling water
1 jar chipped dried beef
   (soaked before using)
3 tablespoons butter
1 tablespoon flour

½ teaspoon pepper
dash of Worcestershire
1 can cream of mushroom
   soup
½ cup sliced olives

Cover dried beef with boiling water and let stand 60 minutes. In a pan melt butter; then stir in flour, pepper, Worcestershire sauce, and soup. Drain water off beef, then add to sauce. Blend in olives. Heat through and serve over toast (or leftover pancakes).

CORNED BEEF 'N CABBAGE CASSEROLE

1 can corned beef, flaked
1 can cream of celery soup
1 onion, chopped

1 teaspoon dry mustard
4 cups cabbage, coarsely
   shredded

Mix all ingredients and put in a baking dish. Cover and bake for 40 minutes at 375 degrees.

STOVE TOP
Place a flame tamer under the skillet and cook at a low heat for 30 to 35 minutes.

PAD THAI NOODLES

3 tablespoons oil	2 teaspoons fish sauce
½ onion, minced	(soy sauce will do)
3 cloves garlic, minced	½ teaspoon sugar
1 egg	salt and pepper to taste
½ pound raw shrimp (opt.)	1 teaspoon tamarind (opt.)
1 package Thai rice noodles	1 cup bean sprouts, optional
(soaked for 5-10 mins.)	¼ cup chopped peanuts
1 cup firm tofu,	as garnish
cut in small pieces	

In a large skillet heat 3 tablespoons oil. Quickly sauté the onion and garlic, then add the egg. Mix, it will cook fast. Next add the shrimp and sauté until they're pink, a few minutes. Add the drained noodles, tofu, spices, fish sauce (or soy sauce) and bean sprouts. Stir together until heated through. Sprinkle with peanuts. Dig in.

SWEET & SOUR HAM

1 tablespoon oil
1 onion, cut in chunks
1 bell pepper, cut in chunks
2 cups ham, cut bite-size

1 small can pineapple
   chunks, drained
1 can sweet & sour sauce

Heat oil in a skillet or wok. Quickly sauté onion and bell pepper, then set aside on a plate. Add a dash of oil and sauté the ham. Add cooked vegetables, pineapple and sweet and sour sauce to the ham and stir to blend ingredients. Simmer for 3 to 5 minutes. Serve over cooked rice.

BEEF SUKIYAKI

2 tablespoons oil
1 pound thinly sliced beef
1 package tofu, cubed

1 cup green onion, diced
1 can bamboo shoots
1 package mung bean
   noodles, soaked

SUKIYAKI SAUCE
1 cup water
½ cup white wine or sherry

2 teaspoons sugar
¼ cup soy sauce

In a large skillet heat 2 tablespoons oil, quickly sauté the beef slices. Next add all other ingredients. Pour in sauce and stir together. Cook for several minutes. Serve with rice as a side dish.

CORN DOG

oil for deep frying
1 egg
½ cup milk
1 cup biscuit mix
2 tablespoons corn meal

¼ teaspoon paprika
½ teaspoon dry mustard
dash of cayenne
8 to 10 hot dogs
wood skewers
   (inserted in hot dogs)

Heat about 1½ to 2 inches of oil for deep frying. Blend the egg and milk in a bowl, then stir in dry ingredients. Dip the hot dogs into the batter. Fry until golden brown, about 2 to 3 minutes, turning to brown evenly. Serve with prepared mustard.

CURRIED CHICKEN PILAF

¼ cup butter
1½ cups rice (uncooked)
¼ cup onion, diced
2 tablespoons raisins
*2 cans white chicken meat

¼ teaspoon powdered ginger
2 teaspoons curry powder
salt and pepper to taste
3 cups water OR
1½ cups water plus
1½ cups chicken broth

Melt butter in a skillet. Add rice and onion and cook until lightly browned. Add remaining ingredients and 3 cups of water (or a combo of water and chicken broth). Bring to boil, then simmer till rice is cooked. Fluff with a fork and serve immediately.
* OK to use fresh chicken if available.

PRONTO ARROZ CON POLLO
(QUICK CHICKEN WITH RICE)

1 package Spanish rice
3 cans chicken meat
1 can peas, drained
1 can tomatoes,
   drained and chopped

1 jar pimientos, drained
1 small can sliced black olives
1 teaspoon salt and pepper
¼ teaspoon saffron (optional)
¾ cup water

Prepare rice according to package directions. If using whole canned chicken, remove meat from bones. In a skillet combine peas, tomatoes, pimientos, olives, chicken and spices. Add ¾ cup of water (or broth from the canned chicken), bring to a boil, then remove from heat. Add the cooked Spanish rice into the chicken mixture and let stand for 5 minutes. Fluff with a fork, then serve "pronto."

NOODLE WITH CHICKEN SURPRISE

3 to 4 cups cooked noodles
1 can condensed
   cream of celery soup
¼ cup chopped onion
¼ cup chopped bell pepper
1 small jar pimiento

¼ cup chicken bouillon
1 cup Mozzarella cheese,
   grated
2 cans chicken meat
salt and pepper to taste
½ cup bread crumbs

Cook noodles according to package directions. Put cooked noodles and remaining ingredients in a large skillet and lightly mix. Sprinkle some bread crumbs on top. Cook over a low heat for 20 minutes. A heat deflector placed on top of stove burner will prevent ingredients from sticking. If an oven is available, you can put noodle mixture in a greased casserole and bake at 350 degrees for 20 to 25 minutes.

CAN TO PAN COOKERY

STIR-FRY ORIENTAL TURKEY

2 tablespoons oil
1 cup celery, sliced diagonally
1 onion, chopped
1 bell pepper, cut in strips
½ lb. snow peas (or any other similar vegetable)
1 can mushrooms, drained
3 tablespoons chicken broth or water
1 to 2 tablespoons soy sauce
cornstarch to thicken (optional)
2 cans boned turkey or chicken
1 can water chestnuts or bamboo shoots

In a skillet heat 2 tablespoons of oil. Quickly sauté the
celery, onion, bell pepper, snow peas, and mushrooms
until barely tender. Add broth and soy sauce and heat until
bubbly. If runny, thicken with cornstarch. Stir in chicken or
turkey and water chestnuts and heat through.

SPAGHETTI CARBONARA

*Although the ingredients may sound unusual, the results will
change your mind.*

1 (1 lb.) pkg. spaghetti, cooked
   according to directions
½ lb. cooked bacon, crumbled
   (reserve 2 tbsp. drippings)

3 eggs, lightly beaten
1 teaspoon garlic powder
salt and pepper to taste
½ cup grated Parmesan
   cheese

Quickly toss hot, drained spaghetti with reserved bacon
drippings. Then mix in eggs, spices, and cheese. Sprinkle
with crumbled bacon. Serve promptly.

BARBEQUE ORANGE CHICKEN IN FOIL

chicken breasts or thighs
salt and pepper to taste
¼ cup butter

½ cup frozen orange juice
concentrate, thawed
½ teaspoon ginger
chopped parsley (optional)

Place chicken pieces on squares of aluminum foil and sprinkle with salt and pepper. In a saucepan melt butter. Add orange juice concentrate and ginger, stirring until blended. Pour over chicken, then sprinkle with parsley. Seal foil around edges. Place on grill about 5 inches above white-hot coals. Cook about 10 minutes until chicken is no longer pink.

INDIAN-STYLE CHICKEN CURRY

2 tablespoons oil
1 onion, chopped in chunks
1 bell or red pepper cut in strips
1 clove garlic minced
2 cans chicken meat or sliced
chicken breasts (1-2 cups)

2 teaspoons curry powder
½ cup chicken bouillon
1 tomato, cut bite-size
cornstarch to thicken
dash of soy sauce

In a skillet heat oil and sauté the onion, pepper, and garlic. Add chicken and curry powder and stir for one minute. Slowly add broth, and simmer for several minutes. Stir in tomato. Thicken with cornstarch if desired. Season with a dash of soy sauce. Cook till veggies are tender. Serve over rice if desired.

CHICKEN 'N DUMPLINGS

2 teaspoons oil
½ cup chopped onion
½ cup chopped celery
4 boneless chicken breasts,
    sliced

3 cups chicken broth
salt and pepper to taste
1 tablespoon dried parsley
2 cups biscuit mix
¾ cup milk

In a pot sauté onion and celery in oil for a few minutes.
Then add the chicken slices and cook a few more minutes.
Add chicken broth and spices; cook till heated through.
Meanwhile, stir biscuit mix with milk. Drop batter by
tablespoonfuls into boiling chicken. Lower heat and
simmer with lid on for 20 minutes.

CHICKEN TAMALE PIE

1 can Cheddar cheese soup
1 (8 ounce) can tomato sauce
1 cup water
1 to 2 cans white chicken

1 can whole corn, drained
¾ cup uncooked instant rice
1 teaspoon Mexican seasoning
2 large cans tamales

In a large skillet combine soup, tomato sauce, water,
chicken, corn and rice. Sprinkle on Mexican seasoning.
Cover and simmer for 5 minutes. Place tamales on top of
mixture, and continue cooking until tamales are heated
through (about 10 minutes).

SHORT-CUT STUFFED PEPPERS

4 large bell peppers, cut in half
1 tablespoon oil
1 onion chopped
1 (8 ounces) can tomatoes, drained and chopped
1 teaspoon oregano
1 teaspoon basil
1 teaspoon garlic powder
2 (15 ounce) cans macaroni & beef in tomato sauce
½ cup grated mozzarella or Monterey cheese

Remove membrane and seeds from bell pepper halves.
Plunge bell pepper in boiling water for several minutes.
Drain and set aside. Heat one tablespoon oil in a skillet
and sauté the onion, then add the tomatoes, spices, and
macaroni & beef. Stir together, then simmer for 10
minutes. Set bell pepper halves in a baking dish, then stuff
them with macaroni mixture. Top with cheese. Bake at 400
degrees for 15 minutes.

THAI CHICKEN IN GREEN CURRY SAUCE

1 pound boneless, skinless chicken breasts, cut in chunks
2 teaspoons canola oil
salt and pepper to taste
1 to 2 cups sliced green beans, or broccoli
1 can Thai Green Curry sauce

In a skillet sauté the chicken breast in oil until tender.
Season with salt and pepper to taste. Add the canned or
fresh vegetables and the Thai curry sauce. Heat till veggies
are tender. Serve with basmati rice.

.

CHICKEN LOAF & PIMIENTO SAUCE

1 cup bran cereal
¾ cup buttermilk
2 tablespoons celery, chopped
salt and pepper to taste
2 eggs, lightly beaten
½ onion, chopped
1 clove garlic minced
2 cans white chicken meat (or 2 cups cooked chicken)

Mix all ingredients and turn into a greased loaf pan. Bake at 350 degrees for 30 to 40 minutes, or till firm. Serve with sauce spooned over. Or you can mix above ingredients and heat in a skillet.

PARSLEY-PIMIENTO SAUCE

1 tablespoon butter
1 tablespoon flour
¾ cup milk
1 jar pimiento

1 teaspoon lemon juice
2 tablespoons minced parsley
salt and pepper to taste

Melt butter; add flour and stir till smooth. Add milk and continue stirring till sauce thickens. Add remaining ingredients; taste and adjust seasoning. Makes about 1 cup.

CHICKEN TETRAZZINI IN-A-HURRY

1 (6 oz.) package spaghetti
1 onion, chopped
2 tablespoons oil
1 can mushrooms, drained
1 can cream of chicken soup

1½ soup cans milk or cream
¼ cup sherry
2 cans white chicken meat
salt and pepper to taste
1 cup sharp cheese, grated

Cook spaghetti according to package directions. While it cooks, sauté onion in 2 tablespoons oil until tender. Add remaining ingredients, except spaghetti and cheese. Add spaghetti and lightly toss to combine ingredients. Put mixture into a greased casserole and sprinkle with cheese. Bake at 350 degrees for 40 minutes.

NOTE: Remember, a dutch oven or heat deflector placed on stove burner can be substituted for an oven.

TUNA PATTIES WITH CHEESE SAUCE

1½ cups instant mashed potatoes
1 cup water
1 teaspoon butter
1 egg, slightly beaten
1 teaspoon lemon juice
1 can tuna, drained

¼ cup celery, chopped
¼ cup onion, chopped
¼ cup bell pepper,
   chopped
salt and pepper to taste
1 package cheese sauce
   mix

Cook potatoes following package directions but using 1 cup water plus 1 teaspoon butter. After potatoes are cooked, add the egg and lemon juice and blend well. Stir in tuna, celery, onion, and bell pepper. Season to taste with salt and pepper. Following directions, prepare packaged cheese sauce. Heat cheese sauce in a separate pan. Shape mixture into 8 patties and fry about 4 minutes on each side in hot oil. Spoon hot cheese over patties and serve immediately.

ARTICHOKE & CLAM CASSEROLE

1 jar (6 oz.) marinated artichoke
  hearts (reserve marinade)
½ cup chopped onion
¼ cup flour
1 (6 oz.) can minced or chopped
  clams (reserve liquid)
¾ cup milk

1 teaspoon prepared
  mustard
salt & pepper to taste
1 cup bread crumbs
3 tablespoons butter
½ teaspoon parsley
½ teaspoon dill weed

Sauté onion in 2 tablespoons of artichoke marinade. Blend
in flour. Drain liquid from clams into measuring cup, then
add milk to measure 1¼ cup. Stir this into onion mixture,
and cook until mixture thickens. Add mustard, salt,
pepper, and clams. Turn into a baking dish, then sprinkle
on the bread crumbs, pats of butter, parsley, and dill. Bake
at 400 degrees for 15 to 20 minutes or *continue cooking* in
dutch oven over a medium-low heat for 20 to 30 minutes.
VARIATION: Substitute shrimp (4½ oz. can) for clams. Do
not use liquid from canned shrimp for the sauce.

SPAGHETTI WITH CLAM SAUCE

1 pound cooked spaghetti
¼ pound butter
½ onion, chopped
1 tablespoon parsley flakes
½ teaspoon salt
½ teaspoon basil

½ teaspoon oregano
1 tablespoon garlic powder
¼ cup white wine
3 cans chopped clams, drained

Cook spaghetti according to directions on package; drain
water. Melt butter in a skillet and sauté the onion and
parsley flakes. Add the seasonings and wine and simmer
till thoroughly heated. Add the clams, but DO NOT COOK.
Remove from heat. Pour the clam sauce over spaghetti and
serve immediately.

SPANISH TUNA PILAF

1 package Spanish Rice mix
2¼ cups water
1 tablespoon Worcestershire
1 tablespoon butter

¼ onion, chopped
1 can mixed vegetables,
  drained
1 can tuna, drained

In a large skillet combine the rice and 2¼ cups water. Add
the Worcestershire sauce, butter, and onion and bring to a
boil. Reduce heat and simmer with lid on for 20 minutes.
Add vegetables and tuna. Continue cooking for 8 minutes.

BARBECUE FISH IN FOIL

1 pound fish fillets
2 tomatoes, cut in quarters
½ onion, sliced
½ bell pepper, sliced

salt and pepper to taste
garlic powder to taste
¼ cup butter

Divide fish into four portions and place each portion onto
a square of aluminum foil. Top with tomatoes, onion, bell
pepper, seasonings and butter. Fold foil over edges and
ends. Place on grill about 4 inches above white-hot coals.
Cook for about 20 minutes or until the fish flakes.
Serve with lemon wedge.

THAI TUNA CRUNCH CASSEROLE

1 onion, chopped
½ cup celery, chopped
1 can bamboo shoots,
  drained

1 can tuna, drained
1 can Thai Red Curry Sauce
soy sauce to taste
1 cup chopped peanuts

In a large skillet quickly sauté onion, celery, and bamboo
shoots till barely tender. Add remaining ingredients except
peanuts. Simmer over low heat for 5-10 minutes. Top with
chopped peanuts.

10 MINUTE ITALIAN FISH

Even non-seafood eaters will find this dish palatable. The delicate sauce eliminates any fishy odors that often cause people to turn up their noses.

½ cup onion, chopped	1 cup Marinara sauce
¼ cup celery, chopped	salt and pepper to taste
½ cup carrots, sliced	garlic powder to taste
1 pound mild fish fillet	splash of wine, red or white

In a pan sauté onion, celery, and carrots until just tender. Add fish and cover with Italian sauce. Sprinkle with seasonings and add splash of wine. Cook for 10 minutes or until fish flakes.

FISH STEW

1 onion, chopped	garlic powder to taste
½ cup celery, chopped	1 can sliced potatoes, drained
1 can tomatoes, drained	1 can any vegetable, drained
salt and pepper to taste	¼ cup red or white wine
thyme to taste	1 pound white fish, cut in bite-size pieces

In a skillet sauté onion and celery till tender. Stir in tomatoes, spices, potatoes and canned vegetable. Add wine, then fish. Cover and simmer mixture for 10 to 15 minutes until fish is cooked. If a thicker stew is desired, thicken with 2 tablespoons of flour or cornstarch.

FRIED FISH WITH SOUR CREAM SAUCE

1 pound white fish fillets
½ cup cornmeal or
½ cup flour, or ¼ cup of each

salt and pepper to taste
½ cup buttermilk
(see Substitution Chart)

Mix flour and cornmeal. Dip fish in buttermilk, then in cornmeal mixture. Heat ½ inch oil in pan and fry fish on both sides till golden brown. Serve with sour cream sauce.

SOUR CREAM SAUCE
1 cup sour cream
3 tablespoons chopped olives
salt, pepper, paprika to taste

2 tablespoons buttermilk
2 tablespoons parsley

Combine all ingredients and let stand for 30 minutes till flavors blend. Spoon over cooked fish. See SUBSTITUTION CHART for improvising buttermilk.

FISH TERIYAKI

MARINADE
¾ cup water
¾ cup soy sauce
1 teaspoon sugar
1 lb. white fish fillet,
   cut bite-size
2 tablespoons oil

2 cloves garlic
2 teaspoons fresh grated ginger
OR 1½ tablespoons ginger powder
1 onion, cut in chunks
1 bell pepper, cut in chunks
1 tomato, cut in bite-size pieces

Mix marinade in a large bowl and add fish. Let sit in refrigerator for 2 hours. In a large skillet or wok heat 2 tablespoons oil and quickly sauté the onion and bell pepper until barely tender. Add fish and about ½ cup of marinade to the skillet and constantly stir the mixture. The fish will be cooked (when it easily flakes) within 3 to 5 minutes. About one minute before it is done, add the tomatoes and blend in with other ingredients. Serve with hot cooked rice.

Soups

SOUP OF THE SEA

½ cup chopped celery   1 can mackerel
½ cup chopped onion   1 can corn
2 tablespoons oil or butter   1 soup can milk
1 can cream of potato soup   salt, pepper, garlic powder
                                          to taste

In a large pot sauté celery and onion in 2 tablespoons oil or butter. Add remaining ingredients and bring to boil. Reduce heat and simmer for 10 to 15 minutes. Serve immediately with hot French bread.

CREAM OF CONGLOMERATION SOUP

1 can condensed tomato soup
1 can condensed green pea soup
1 soup can water
1 cup milk
2 tablespoons sherry or brandy
2 teaspoons Worcestershire sauce or lamon juice
1 can shrimp, drained

Combine soups in saucepan, then add water and milk, mixing until smooth. Slowly bring to boil, stirring frequently. Add brandy, Worcestershire, and shrimp. Heat another 2 minutes. Serve piping hot.

BUTTERNUT SQUASH SOUP

1 butternut squash, chopped	4 cans chicken broth
1 cup celery, chopped	half & half or milk
1 cup carrot, chopped	salt and pepper to taste
1 apple, chopped	

In a pot combine the squash, celery, carrot, and apple, then add the chicken broth. Cook until the vegetables are tender, stirring occasionally. Add enough half and half or milk to make a desired consistency. Serve piping hot.

POTATO-CHEESE SOUP

2 teaspoons oil	1 tablespoon parsley
1 onion, chopped	1 can tomatoes and liquid
½ cup celery, chopped	1 cup Cheddar cheese, shredded
2 cups water	¼ cup butter
2 cups milk	¼ cup flour
1 can sliced potatoes, drained	salt and pepper to taste
	½ teaspoon dry mustard
	½ teaspoon Worcestershire sauce

In a large pot, sauté onion and celery in oil until tender. Add water and milk, bring to boil, then reduce heat. Add potatoes, parsley, tomatoes, and cheese.
In a saucepan melt butter, then blend in flour, salt, pepper, mustard, and Worcestershire sauce. Stir flour mixture into soup and heat for 10 minutes. Serve immediately.

CORN & BEAN SOUP

1 tablespoon oil or butter	1 can white chicken meat
1 onion, chopped	salt and pepper to taste
1 can navy beans	oregano to taste
2 cans chicken broth	cumin to taste
1 can diced green chiles	garlic powder to taste
1 can white hominy	parsley flakes for garnish
	½ cup shredded Cheddar cheese

In a pot sauté onion in 1 tablespoon oil or butter. Add the beans, chicken broth, chiles, hominy, chicken and spices. Simmer soup for 15 minutes, then stir in the cheese. Serve with tortillas.

MEAL-IN-A-POT MINESTRONE

Today's busy cooks don't have time to simmer and stir homemade soups, yet they still want the robust flavor like Mom used to make ... so here ya go.

l teaspoon vegetable oil
l onion, sliced
1 to 3 cloves garlic, minced (or 1 teaspoon garlic powder)
½ cup each carrots and bell pepper, minced
2 cups cabbage, shredded
  OR l cup zucchini, chopped
½ cup kidney or garbanzo beans (optional)
1 (16 ounce) can whole tomatoes, broken up
*1 to 2 cooked and crumbled Italian sausage (optional)
1 cup egg noodles, broken in small pieces
    OR 1½ cup leftover cooked rice or pasta
2 teaspoons Italian spices
salt and pepper to taste
2 cans (10½ ounce) beef broth or chicken broth
l jar (15 ounce) spaghetti sauce

In a pot, heat the oil and quickly sauté the onion and garlic. Add the carrots, bell pepper, cabbage (or zucchini) and sauté for a few minutes. Blend in all the other ingredients, including the liquid from the canned tomatoes, and simmer for 15 minutes or until heated through. Add the noodles and simmer for 7 more minutes. Serve immediately with hot garlic bread.

CURRIED CREAM-OF-CHICKEN SOUP

⅓ cup celery, chopped
1 onion, chopped
2 tablespoons butter

1 teaspoon curry powder
2 cans cream of chicken soup
2 soup cans milk

Sauté celery and onion in butter. Stir in curry powder; add soup and milk. Heat and serve. Makes 5 cups.

HEARTY CHICKEN SOUP

1 tablespoon oil
½ cup onion chopped
2 cans chicken broth
1 can water chestnuts or bamboo shoots, drained
1 cup cooked rice
1 cup cooked chicken
1 can mushrooms
1 teaspoon soy sauce

Sauté onion in 1 tablespoon oil. Add the remaining ingredients. Bring to a boil; reduce heat and simmer 10 minutes Garnish with chow mien noodles if desired.

CLAM & TUNA CHOWDER

1 tablespoon oil	1½ cups powdered milk
½ onion, chopped	¼ cup nondairy creamer
4 cups water	OR 1 cup whole milk or
1 can potatoes, drained, cubed	half & half
1 can tuna, drained	½ teaspoon seasoned salt
1 can minced clams, undrained	½ teaspoon pepper
	½ teaspoon celery salt
	few dashes Worcestershire

Sauté onion in 1 tablespoon oil. Stir in water, potatoes, tuna, clams, powdered milk, creamer, and seasonings. Bring to a boil, then reduce heat; cover and simmer for 15 minutes.

SOUP COMBINATIONS

Combining two or more canned soups will add new and delicious flavors to your meals. Here are some examples:

cream of mushroom and tomato
black bean and tomato
tomato and clam chowder
tomato and cream-of-celery
clam chowder and green pea
tomato and green pea
clam chowder and vegetable
cream-of-onion and vegetable
tomato and beef noodle
French onion and tomato
cream-of-mushroom and French onion
vegetable and beef (and chicken) noodle
tomato and chicken gumbo

QUICK & THICK CLAM CHOWDER

1 can clam chowder, Manhattan style
1 (6½ ounce) can clams
I can stewed tomatoes

Pour chowder, clams and their liquid, and stewed tomatoes into a pan. Do not add additional liquid as soup can instructs. Stir and heat.

MORE HELPFUL HINTS

11. For an emergency coffee filter, fit an ordinary, unscented facial tissue into the coffee basket.

12. Avocados will ripen faster in a tightly closed brown paper bag.

13. For delicious flavor, add an orange peel to the teapot a few minutes before serving.

14. Use leftover coffee in place of liquid when making tapioca pudding. Add extra sugar and a tablespoon of chocolate syrup to create a mocha flavor.

15. Extend scrambled eggs with that last dab of leftover cottage cheese. (Two tablespoons cottage cheese replaces one egg.)

16. Improvise carbonated drinks by using half a glass of fruit juice and filling the rest with club soda.

17. Use leftover dill pickle juice to marinate carrot sticks: marinate overnight or longer and serve with cocktails.

18. When cooking rice, double the portion and use the cooked rice in meatloaf in place of breadcrumbs, or in cold salads, or make rice pancakes (use one cup rice for one cup flour).

19. An easy way to drain canned food liquid is to first puncture the top and spill off excess liquid before fully opening the container.

20. For short day excursions take along hot dogs in a thermos jug filled with boiling water. Don't forget the buns.

For the entire list of helpful hints, see Appendix p. 142.

Salads

MARINATED BEAN SALAD

1 can green beans, drained	½ onion, sliced thin
1 can kidney beans, drained	¼ cup vinegar
1 can wax beans, optional	½ cup oil
	salt and pepper to taste

Mix all ingredients in a bowl and chill for 1 to 2 hours before serving. NOTE: Wax beans can be substituted for green beans.

TABOULI SALAD (CRACKED WHEAT, ALA)

1 cup cracked wheat	1 tomato, chopped
2 cups hot water	1 cup onion, chopped
1 cup parsley (fresh)	1 cucumber, chopped
1 cup celery (optional)	¼ cup fresh lemon juice
½ cup oil	salt, pepper, and garlic powder to taste

Soak the cracked wheat in 2 cups hot water for 20 minutes. When water is absorbed, add other ingredients to the cracked wheat, stirring to blend evenly. Let flavors blend before serving.

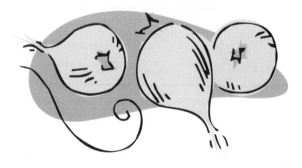

UNCANNY POTATO SALAD

1 can sliced potatoes, drained
2 teaspoons bell pepper, chopped
1 hard-boiled egg, crumbled
1 teaspoon mustard
¼ cup onion, diced
½ cup mayonnaise
1 teaspoon chopped pickle, optional
salt and pepper to taste

Combine all ingredients and gently stir until well blended.
Chill at least one hour before serving.

CREAMY BEET SALAD

1 large can beets, drained & sliced
¾ cup plain yogurt
1 to 2 tablespoons prepared horseradish

Combine yogurt and horseradish, then stir in beets. Chill one
hour before serving.

HASH BROWN POTATO SALAD

1 pkg. instant hash brown potatoes   ½ cup celery
1 cup chicken broth   ½ cup bell pepper, chopped
½ cup chopped onion   1 cup mayonnaise

Reconstitute hash browns according to package directions but
use chicken broth in place of water. When liquid is absorbed,
let hash browns cool. In a bowl combine the potatoes and
remaining ingredients. Season with salt and pepper. Chill 1
hour before serving.

NO MAYO POTATO SALAD

Calorie counters may be interested to know that a cup of sour cream has 485 calories. But plain yogurt, which is an excellent substitute, contains only 150 calories per cup. A medium potato has 90 calories. Mayonnaise has a staggering 1,587 calories per cup compared to imitation mayonnaise, which has one-third the calories. Conclusion: when you're having a potato salad attack, try this recipe and avoid guilt feelings.

½ cup chopped onion   1 or 2 hard-boiled eggs, crumbled
½ cup chopped celery   2 to 3 cups cooked potatoes, cubed
salt and pepper to taste   OR
1 cup plain yogurt   2 cans sliced potatoes, drained
1 teaspoon prepared mustard

In a large bowl combine onion, celery, salt, pepper, yogurt and mustard and mix well. Fold in eggs and potatoes and gently toss. Chill for 1 hour before serving.

APPLE-BEET SALAD

1 large can beets, drained and diced
⅓ cup pickle relish (optional)
¼ cup chopped onion
2 tablespoons vinegar
1 teaspoon sugar
½ cup mayonnaise
1 apple, diced
salt and pepper to taste

Combine ingredients and gently toss to mix. Chill 1 hour before serving.

QUICK ANTIPASTO

1 pint jar Giardiniera vegetables, drained
2 (6 ounce) jars marinated artichoke hearts, undrained
1 (8 ounce) jar button mushrooms, drained
1 (8 ounce) jar pitted black olives, drained
2 (8 ounce) cans tomato sauce
1 (7½ ounce) can water-packed tuna, drained
4 tablespoons vinegar

Combine all ingredients and mix well. Refrigerate for 12 hours or more. Stir before serving.

SAUERKRAUT SALAD

1 large can sauerkraut, drained
1 cup chopped apple

1 cup minced onion
1 cup minced green pepper
¼ cup sugar
½ cup vinegar

Mix together the sauerkraut, minced onion, minced green pepper, and chopped apple. Boil the sugar and vinegar, then pour over the other ingredients. Chill for several hours.

CUCUMBER AND SHRIMP SALAD

This Japanese recipe is quite palatable to Americans.

½ cup water
¼ cup vinegar
2 tablespoons soy sauce
1 teaspoon sugar
1 large cucumber, sliced paper thin
1 can shrimp, drained

In a bowl combine water, vinegar, soy sauce, and sugar. Stir in cucumbers. Cover and chill for an hour or two.

ORANGE COLESLAW

1 cup mayonnaise
1 tablespoon sugar
2 teaspoon vinegar
4 cups shredded cabbage
1 (11 ounce) can mandarin oranges, drained

Combine mayonnaise, sugar and vinegar; add to cabbage. Mix well. Add orange segments, mix to combine.

CANTALOUPE, JICAMA, & CUCUMBER SALAD

1 cantaloupe, cut in cubes
2 cups peeled & cubed jicama
1 large cucumber, cut in cubes
⅓ cup fresh lemon juice

1 teaspoon chile powder
salt & pepper to taste
¼ cup cilantro, minced

Combine ingredients and gently toss to mix. Chill 1 hour before serving.

RAW CAULIFLOWER SALAD

Cauliflower will last several days without refrigeration, and it makes a nice crunchy salad.

1 cup mayonnaise   1 med. head cauliflower flowerets
1 onion, diced   1 can green peas, drained
3 to 4 tablespoons milk ½ cup chopped celery, optional
½ teaspoon each salt and pepper

In a bowl, mix mayonnaise, onion, milk, salt and pepper. Break cauliflower into florets; add celery and peas to mayonnaise mixture. Toss lightly and chill.

FRESH MUSHROOM SALAD

½ lb. mushrooms, sliced thin ½ cup diced celery (optional)
½ onion, sliced thin   ¼ cup lemon juice (or
½ cup oil   vinegar)
salt, pepper, garlic powder to taste

Put all ingredients in a bowl and gently toss. Chill for several hours before serving.

QUICKY SHRIMP COCKTAIL

1 cup ketchup or chili sauce
1 tablespoon horseradish
1 can shrimp, drained
   (1 pound fresh shrimp is much better)
lettuce leaves
lemon wedges (optional)

Combine 1 cup of cocktail sauce (or ketchup) with 1
tablespoon horseradish. Stir to blend, adding more
horseradish if you like heat. Arrange shrimp on a plate lined
with lettuce leaves and top with sauce. Serve with lemon
wedges. Chill before serving.

ARTICHOKE SALAD

1 jar marinated artichoke hearts (reserve marinade)
1 tablespoon oil
½ onion, chopped
1 can water chestnuts, sliced
1 jar sliced mushrooms
1 teaspoon vinegar
dash of Worcestershire sauce

Combine all ingredients, including marinade from
artichoke hearts. Gently toss until all ingredients are coated.
Chill before serving.

CAN TO PAN COOKERY

SHRIMP & MACARONI SALAD

2 cups raw macaroni (cooked per directions on package)
1 can shrimp, drained
1 chopped onion
1 can chopped black olives
1 cup mayonnaise
1 hard-cooked egg, crumbled
salt, pepper, mustard powder to taste

Cool macaroni, drain, then stir in all other ingredients and seasonings to taste. Toss and blend together; chill before serving.

SHRIMP OR CRAB LOUIE

It's amazing how delicious canned shrimp, or crab, tastes in a salad.

1 can shrimp or crab, drained
OR 1 package imitation crab/shrimp
2 hard-cooked eggs, sliced thin
1 tomato, cut in wedges
1 head Romaine or leaf lettuce, torn in bite-size pieces
1 avocado, cut in wedges

Gently toss all ingredients in a large salad bowl. Top with your favorite salad dressing—Thousand Island is traditional.

RICE AND ARTICHOKE SALAD

1 package chicken Rice-A-Roni
2 green onions, sliced
½ bell pepper, chopped
8 pimiento olives, chopped (optional)
2 (6 oz.) jars marinated artichoke hearts, reserve marinade
⅓ cup mayonnaise
¼ teaspoon curry powder

Cook rice according to package directions, then cool. In a
bowl add cooled rice, onion, pepper, olives, and artichoke
hearts. Blend in marinade, mayonnaise, and curry powder,
then toss well. Refrigerate and allow flavors to blend for
several hours.

AMBROSIA SALAD

1 cup sour cream (reg. or lite)
2 cups miniature marshmallows
2 cans mandarin oranges
1 small jar cherries, sliced
1 small can pineapple
   chunks
sugar to taste

Put sour cream in a bowl. Using a fork, blend in other
ingredients. Chill for several hours before serving.

RICE & BEAN SALAD

*Wondering how to use leftover rice? Try this rice and bean
salad for a pleasant surprise.*

1 cup cooked rice
1 can (16 oz.) kidney or
   pinto beans, drained
2 hard-boiled eggs, chopped
1 small onion, diced
¼ cup pickle relish
¼ cup mayonnaise
salt and pepper to taste

Mix all ingredients and let flavors blend about one hour before serving. NOTE: For best flavors, combine while rice is hot.

GREEN BEAN SALAD

1 (16 ounce) can green beans, drained
¼ onion, sliced thin
1 tomato, cubed (optional)
Italian Dressing

Combine ingredients in a bowl and mix well.

CHINESE COLESLAW

1 small head cabbage, shredded
1 can shrimp, drained
Or 1 package Imo-refrigerated shrimp meat
4 chopped green onions
½ cup cilantro, chopped (optional)
½ cup shredded carrots (optional)

DRESSING
½ cup mayonnaise
2 teaspoons soy sauce
½ teaspoon ground ginger
½ teaspoon garlic powder

Put cabbage, shrimp, green onions and cilantro in a bowl, then toss with dressing. Chill before serving.

EVEN MORE HELPFUL HINTS

21. Biscuit mix is excellent for breading meats or fish. Use instead of flour or bread crumbs.

22. For variety, make sandwiches using pancakes or waffles (leftover from breakfast) instead of bread. Pita bread, waffles, and tortillas are great too.

23. Add a beaten egg to hot chicken soup for extra nutrition.

24. Don't discard an old fork; bend back the prongs and use to neatly remove pickles from their jars.

25. If you need to soak dried fruit such as prunes or apricots, they'll be more flavorful if soaked in cold tea.

26. No candleholders for a romantic picnic dinner? Core a rosy apple or even an orange and put a candle down the hole.

27. Save time starting a barbecue fire by placing charcoal briquettes into each compartment of a cardboard egg carton. Close the carton and light.

28. When a recipe requires a stove-top casserole be finished in the oven, protect skillet handles from burning by wrapping them in aluminum foil.

29. To liven up canned fruit cocktail, add a shot of rum or brandy an hour before serving. Garnish with miniature marshmallows.

30. Don't forget the "crunch" in menu planning. People psychologically need to get their teeth into something chewy to get that soul-satisfying crunch sound.

(For the entire list of helpful hints, see Appendix p. 142.)

CAN TO PAN COOKERY

Vegetables

BARBECUED CORN

Place individual ears of clean corn in a square of foil. Before sealing, add an ice cube and pat of butter. Place wrapped corn directly on the coals. Turn frequently to prevent burnt spots. OR...lay the corn in its husk on top of the hot grill. Turn frequently. When cooked through, husk the corn and dig in.

GLAZED CARROTS

1 pound raw carrots, sliced
3 tablespoons butter
1 tablespoons brown sugar

Melt butter in a skillet, then add the sliced carrots. Stir in the brown sugar. Add water as the carrots cook to prevent from sticking to the pan. When carrots are tender crisp, they're ready.

BARBECUED POTATOES & ONION

2 potatoes, sliced
1 onion, sliced
(double for a larger serving)
salt and pepper to taste

Before wrapping the potatoes and onions in aluminum foil, sprinkle with salt and pepper. Seal the foil and place directly on coals. Turn occasionally to prevent burning. Should be ready in 20 to 25 minutes, or when potatoes are soft.

OVENLESS BAKED POTATOES

1 potato per person (washed and cleaned)
vegetable oil

Lightly coat each potato with vegetable oil. If the potato is large, cut in half to shorten cooking time.

PRESSURE COOKER
Put 1 cup of water into cooker, place rack in bottom, then put potatoes on top of rack. Secure lid and cook for 12 minutes starting AFTER regulator cap begins rattling. Run cool water on lid to quickly drop the pressure, or let it drop on its own.

TABLETOP STOVE
Put potatoes directly on bottom of tabletop stove and cook for 30 minutes or until potato becomes soft to touch. Turn occasional to prevent burning.

MICROWAVE
Using a fork, poke a few holes in the potato, then wrap each potato in a paper towel. Microwave on high for 7 minutes or until potatoes are soft.

DILLED GREEN BEANS

3 tablespoons butter
1 onion chopped
1 stalk celery, chopped
1 clove garlic, minced

1 tablespoon dried parsley
1 teaspoon dried dill weed
1 can French-cut green beans
salt and pepper to taste

To make dill sauce, melt butter in saucepan and sauté onion, celery, and garlic. Add parsley and dill, simmer 10 minutes; if necessary add ¼ cup water to pan. Add green beans to sauce and simmer until heated through.

HOMINY IN SOUR CREAM

Yankees may not be familiar with hominy, but it's a common dish down South and is often substituted for potatoes.

1 tablespoon butter
1 can hominy, drained

1 cup sour cream
salt and pepper to taste

Melt butter in a skillet, then add hominy. Cover with sour cream, and warm on a low heat. Season with salt and pepper.

SAUTEED MUSHROOMS

Scrumptious companion to steak.

¼ stick butter
1 large can mushrooms, drained
salt, pepper, and garlic powder to taste
2 teaspoons sherry (optional)
1 teaspoon soy sauce

Melt butter in a skillet. Add other ingredients and simmer for 5 minutes. Serve immediately.

HASH BROWNS & CHEESE CASSEROLE

1 pkg. instant hash browns
1 can Cheddar cheese soup

1 small can evaporated milk
1 can French fried onion rings

Follow package directions to reconstitute the hash browns. After potatoes become soft, mix with other ingredients and blend. Pour mixture into a greased baking dish and bake for 30 minutes at 350 degrees.

BAKED TOMATO CASSEROLE

1 pound can tomatoes, drained and sliced
1 small onion, chopped
½ teaspoon each salt and pepper
½ teaspoon each basil & garlic powder
½ cup olive oil
2 cups French bread, cubed & toasted
3 tablespoons Parmesan cheese

In a bowl mix tomatoes, onion, seasonings and oil. In a
baking dish layer with half the toasted bread cubes. Top
with a layer of tomato mixture. Top with remaining bread
cubes and sprinkle with cheese. Bake in a 375 degree oven
for 20 minutes.

BOATSWAIN'S RED CABBAGE

1 red onion, chopped
2 to 3 teaspoons vegetable oil
1 (16 ounce) jar red cabbage
1 cup applesauce
salt, pepper, and vinegar to taste
¼ teaspoon nutmeg

In a skillet sauté the onion until tender. Add the cabbage
and applesauce and heat for 10 minutes. Taste and add the
remaining ingredients.   Cook till heated through.

ASPARAGUS DAWDLER STYLE

In honor of Hal Schell, the "Delta Dawdler."

1 (15½ ounce) can asparagus, drained
1 can cream of mushroom soup
1 cup Cheddar cheese, grated

TOPPING
½ cup crumbled potato chips or bread crumbs

Mix all the ingredients (except topping) and put into a greased loaf pan. Sprinkle topping over mixture. Bake at 350 degrees for 15 minutes. Or heat the entire mixture in a skillet. Before serving, sprinkle on topping.

Baked Goods

COMMENDABLE COBBLER

This worthy dish is always a welcome dessert or snack.

3 to 4 apples, chopped (skin and all)
*¾ cup sugar
1 teaspoon cinnamon
1½ tablespoons butter
1½ cups biscuit mix
1 egg
   (if no egg is available, eliminate it, cobbler will be a bit
   crumbly, but good)
½ cup milk

Grease a medium size baking pan. Add chopped apples,
then cover them with sugar and 1 teaspoon cinnamon; dot
with butter. In a separate bowl mix biscuit mix, egg, and
milk and stir to blend. Don't worry as there will be some
lumps in batter. Drop batter by spoonfuls on apples till they
are covered. Dust with cinnamon. Bake at 350 degrees for
20 minutes.
*OK to use a combination of white and brown sugar.

NO OVEN
Use a tabletop stove. Cooking time will vary, but when a
toothpick comes out clean, it's ready to eat.

PRESSURE COOKER BREAD

1 tablespoon sugar
1 envelope dry yeast
1¼ cup warm salt water OR 1¼ cup water with 1 teaspoon salt
1 envelope dry yeast
4 cups flour

Add sugar and yeast to water. Stir the mixture into the flour. Knead for several minutes till dough is stretchy. Put the dough ball in a bowl and set in a warm spot and let it rise for 1 to 2 hours. After it has risen the first time, remove from the bowl and punch dough down. Now put the dough ball in a greased pressure cooker. You can dust the inside of the pressure cooker with flour or corn meal if you wish. Let the dough rise again. Put the lid on the pressure cooker BUT DO NOT LOWER THE VALVE. Cook over low heat for 30 minutes. Turn bread, cover and cook until bread smells ready (10-20 minutes).

CINNAMON CORNBREAD

1 package corn muffin mix
1 cup raisins
½ cup chopped nuts (optional)
1 teaspoon cinnamon

Follow package
directions but
add raisins, nuts
and cinnamon to
mixture. Serve
with plenty of
butter.

ENGLISH MUFFINS

*Bread is usually the first food you'll run out of on long trips.
Here's a homemade remedy.*

1 tablespoon yeast	1 teaspoon salt
1 cup warm water	¼ cup oil or melted butter
1 cup milk	½ cup cool water
1 tablespoon sugar	3 cups flour

Dissolve yeast in warm water. Combine milk, sugar, salt, oil
(or melted butter), and cool water. Gradually add flour.
Mix until the dough is smooth and elastic. Let rise
for about 1 hour. Roll dough on floured surface to ½"
thickness, then cut into circles with 3" diameter. Cook in a
greased skillet for about seven minutes per side.

QUICK ONION BREAD

1 cup onion, chopped, OR	2 cups biscuit mix
1 can French fried onions	¾ cup milk
½ cup bell pepper, chopped	1 cup sour cream
2 tablespoons butter or oil	salt and pepper to taste
2 eggs	

If using fresh onions, sauté chopped onions and bell pepper
in 1 tablespoon butter or oil. If using canned onions, just
sauté the bell pepper in the oil or butter. Set aside. In
a bowl beat 1 egg, then add biscuit mix and milk. Stir
to blend. Butter a baking dish and pour in biscuit mix
batter. Spread onion/pepper mixture over, leaving ¼ cup
of mixture for topping. Beat remaining egg and add sour
cream; add salt and pepper to taste. Spread over onion/

pepper mix. Sprinkle on remaining onion mixture. Bake at 400 degrees for 25 minutes. Cut into squares and serve.

PAN BREAD
(MADE ON TOP OF THE STOVE)

This is an all-time favorite that is so delicious you'll eat and eat until it's all gone, leaving little room for anything else.

3 cups flour
1 cup sugar
1 teaspoon cinnamon
1 teaspoon vanilla
1 egg

½ cup milk
1½ teaspoons baking powder
½ teaspoon nutmeg
½ cup soft butter

Mix all ingredients in a bowl. Pour into a well greased skillet. Put lid on and cook on top of the stove over a medium flame for about 20 to 30 minutes. Turn over and cook other side until golden brown. Serve immediately with butter.

SPOON BREAD

1½ cups milk
1½ cups cornmeal
1 teaspoon salt
2 eggs beaten

2 tablespoons butter
1 teaspoon sugar
1 teaspoon baking powder

Scald milk. Stir in cornmeal and salt, making a mush. After mush thickens, add eggs, butter, sugar, and baking powder. Pour in a greased baking dish. Bake 30 minutes at 400 degrees.

TORTILLA COOKIE

It's international to have a craving for something sweet. Here's a solution from our neighbors south of the border.

½ stick butter
1 cup brown sugar
1 egg, slightly beaten
½ cup flour
1 teaspoon vanilla
8 flour tortillas, cut in half & lightly buttered
1 cup raisins
1 cup nuts, chopped

Melt butter in a skillet, then blend in brown sugar. Stir in egg, flour, and vanilla. Spread about 1 tablespoon of the mixture in the center of tortilla; sprinkle with raisins and nuts and roll up. Arrange on a cookie sheet. Bake at 375 degrees for 8 to 10 minutes till tortilla is crisp.

WHOLE WHEAT FLOUR TORTILLAS

3 cups wheat flour   ½ teaspoon salt
2 teaspoons baking powder   ¾ to 1 cup warm water

Stir together dry ingredients. Gradually add water to make a crumbly dough. Knead on a floured surface until smooth. Divide into 12 pieces. Roll each ball into a thin tortilla. Cook over a medium-high heat in a slightly greased skillet. Press down with a spatula as blisters appear. Flip over and cook other side.

NEED-NO-KNEAD WHOLE WHEAT BREAD

This hassle-free method sounds too good to be true; but each time you take out a perfectly baked loaf of bread, you'll be reassured this recipe is real.

1 tablespoon honey	1 tablespoon salt
2 tablespoons molasses	1 cup wheat germ
2 cups warm water	1 cup white flour
1 tablespoon yeast	2 cups whole wheat flour

In a bowl put the honey, molasses and warm water. Add yeast and mix thoroughly until it has dissolved; let mixture stand for 5 to 10 minutes. Gradually add the rest of the ingredients. Stir as vigorously as possible. The mixture will be sticky, so don't be alarmed. Put the dough into two small, well-greased loaf pans that should be about half full. Let dough rise to top of pans (about 1 to 1½ hours). Bake at 350 degrees for 50 to 60 minutes, or until crust is dark brown. Brush the top of loaves with butter and cool for 10 minutes before loosening from pans. Cool loaves upside down for 20 minutes before serving, if your crew will wait that long!

SKILLET WHOLE WHEAT BREAD

This quick and easy bread tastes like the "real thing."

1½ cups wheat flour	1 teaspoon baking powder
½ cup white flour	½ teaspoon salt

Mix all ingredients and turn onto a floured surface. Roll dough mixture flat, then cut into 8 (five-inch) circles. Heat a dab of oil in a skillet before adding bread circles. Cook over a medium heat for 2 to 3 minutes on each side. When bread is brown and puffy it's ready. Serve immediately.

CLEAN-UP HINTS

1. Delegate clean-up duties. Immediately write the author if you have a foolproof plan to coerce your crew.
2. Clean and sweeten stainless steel coffee pots and vacuum bottles by placing three tablespoons baking soda into a quart of hot water and letting it stand in the container for 10 minutes. Rinse well.
3. Clean a coffee pot by filling it with soapy water and percolating for 15 minutes.
4. Polish chrome or stainless steel pots with a cloth moistened with white vinegar.
5. To prevent plastic dishware and utensils from becoming stained, add a few drops of bleach into the dishwater. Let heavily stained plasticware soak in a stronger solution for 10 minutes.

(For the entire list of helpful hints, see Appendix p. 142.)

Desserts

PRESSURE COOKER BAKED APPLES

A tasty and quick dessert for lazy days.

1 apple per person (peeled around top)
cinnamon, brown sugar, white sugar
Topping: whipped cream or cream

Place each apple in an individual baking dish with about 1 inch of water. Sprinkle with 1 teaspoon of white and brown sugar (more for a sweeter apple) and about ½ teaspoon cinnamon. Add 1 cup of water to pressure cooker, then put in rack. Place baking dishes on rack and secure lid. Cook apples for 5 minutes (starting after regulator begins rattling). Top with cream and serve immediately.

STUFFED DESSERT PEACHES

3 tablespoons butter
2 teaspoons sugar
¼ teaspoon cinnamon
¼ teaspoon nutmeg
⅓ cup finely chopped dates
  or raisins

⅓ cup chopped nuts
⅓ cup chopped dried
  apricots (optional)
1 can peach halves, drained

In a saucepan melt butter, then add sugar, cinnamon, and nutmeg. Stir well. Add dates, nuts, and apricots and blend in butter mixture. Fill peach halves with about 1 tablespoon of fruit mixture. Chill before serving.

HAYSTACKS

Here's a simple, yummy no-bake cookie treat.

1 (6 ounce) package semisweet chocolate chips
1 (6 ounce) package butterscotch pieces
1 (6 ounce) can chow mein noodles
½ cup chopped nuts (any kind)

Melt chocolate chip and butterscotch pieces. Remove
from heat and quickly stir in chow mein noodles and nuts
and stir until evenly coated. Drop by teaspoonsfuls onto
waxed paper. Chill and store in cool place. Yields about 36
haystacks.

PUDDING PARFAIT

1 package instant pudding, any flavor
1 can fruit cocktail
chopped nuts, garnish

In a parfait glass or similar
container, alternate a layer
of pudding with a layer
of chopped fruit cocktail.
Sprinkle with nuts.

BREAD PUDDING WITH FRUIT

This is an excellent way to use stale bread and overripe fruit.

6 slices bread	½ cup raisins
OR	¼ cup chopped walnuts
2 cups plain cubed stuffing mix	1 cup brown sugar
1 banana, sliced	⅔ cup water
1 apple, cored and diced	½ teaspoon cinnamon

Toast bread and cut in small cubes. In a large mixing bowl, combine bread cubes, banana, apple, raisins, and walnuts. Add brown sugar, water, and cinnamon, tossing to coat evenly. Turn into a medium casserole. Bake uncovered at 325 degrees for 30 to 35 minutes. Serve with cream.

DESSERT DUMPLINGS

This is a fine treat that doesn't take long to prepare.

¼ cup water	½ teaspoon salt
1½ cups maple syrup	2 tablespoons butter
2 cups flour	1 cup plus 2 tablespoons
1 tablespoon baking powder	milk

In a large saucepan (so there will be sufficient room for the dumplings) bring water and syrup to a boil. In a bowl mix flour, baking powder, and salt. Add shortening, then stir in milk. Drop dough by spoonfuls into boiling syrup mixture. Turn down heat. Cover tightly and boil gently 12 to 15 minutes. Serve dumplings with syrup spooned over. Makes about 12 large dumplings.

BANANA FLAMBÉ

People tend to associate flaming desserts with gourmet cooking. Here's a simple yet delicious way to visually impress dinner guests.

4 bananas   1 teaspoon cinnamon
½ cup butter   ¼ cup warmed brandy or rum
¼ cup mixture of white and brown sugar

Peel and halve bananas. In a large skillet, melt butter, then add bananas. Sprinkle the sugar and cinnamon over bananas. Simmer for 10 minutes until bananas are tender. Heat brandy, but do not bring to a boil. Bring the bananas in the skillet to the table, pour heated brandy over them and ignite.

ELEGANT FRUIT & CHEESE SAMPLER

1 orange, peeled and sliced   wedges of Cheddar cheese
1 cup pineapple chunks   and Swiss cheese
2 bananas, sliced
1 apple, sliced

Arrange ingredients on a platter and sprinkle with chopped nuts.

CHOCOLATE DESSERT FONDUE

A unique dessert to serve for chocolate lovers.

1 can (ready-made) chocolate
   frosting
1 tablespoon corn syrup
1 tablespoon milk

Dippers: bite-size pieces of pound cake, apples, strawberries, pretzels, bananas, caramel pieces

Heat frosting, corn syrup and milk in a saucepan over low heat. Stir till blended. While still hot, spear the dippers and swirl in chocolate mixture.

PEACH TRIFLE

1 package (12 ounce) vanilla
   wafers
2 cups instant custard
1 can (1 pound) cling
   peaches, drained and
   sliced

garnish: maraschino cherries and slivered almonds

Starting with wafers, alternately layer the peaches, custard, and wafers, ending with custard on top. Garnish with cherries and slivered almonds. Chill before serving.

CHOCOLATE-BANANA SHORTCAKE

1 package nondairy whipped topping
½ cup chocolate syrup
1 package pound cake, sliced
2 bananas, sliced

Prepare nondairy whipped topping according to package directions. Mix whipped topping with chocolate syrup. On a serving plate start layering with half of the sliced pound cake on the bottom; follow with a thin layer of whipped cream mixture, then add half of the sliced bananas. Build another layer in the same order, ending with sliced bananas on top. Decorate with a dollop of whipped cream mixture. Chill before serving.

PEANUT BUTTER CHOCOLATE PUDDING

2 cups cold milk
¼ cup peanut butter
1 package (4½ ounce) instant chocolate pudding
3 tablespoons chopped peanuts (optional)

Gradually beat milk into peanut butter. Add instant pudding and continue mixing until smooth and somewhat thickened. Pour pudding into dishes, garnish with chopped peanuts, and chill till ready to serve.

BISCUIT BAKED PRUNE

2 cups biscuit mix   ⅓ cup cinnamon/sugar mixture
⅔ cups milk   ½ cup melted butter
2 cups pitted prunes

Combine and stir biscuit mix and milk until it becomes a dough. Wrap prunes in biscuit dough. Arrange on a lightly greased cookie sheet and sprinkle with cinnamon/sugar mixture. Bake at 450 degrees for 10 to 12 minutes. While still hot, brush with melted butter.

MACARONI PUDDING

2 cups milk	½ cup raisins
½ cup uncooked macaroni	½ teaspoon nutmeg
2 eggs	1 teaspoon vanilla
¼ cup sugar	1 teaspoon grated lemon peel

Heat, but do not boil, milk. Add macaroni and simmer until tender. Beat eggs, add sugar, and stir until thick. Combine egg mixture with milk and macaroni; add raisins, nutmeg, vanilla, and lemon peel. Pour into a greased baking pan and bake for 45 minutes at 300 degrees. Serve warm with sour cream. Variation: Omit raisins and use dates, figs, dried apricots, or pitted prunes.

PLUM PUDDING WITH HARD SAUCE

You don't have to wait for Christmas to enjoy the festive flavor of plum pudding.

1 can Crosse & Blackwell plum pudding (heated or steamed)

HARD SAUCE

⅓ cup butter	½ teaspoon vanilla
1 cup powdered sugar	1 teaspoon brandy (optional)

Cream butter. Add powdered sugar and continue beating. Add vanilla and brandy and continue beating until fluffy. Serve immediately or keep chilled. Top the warmed plum pudding with hard sauce. Note: Canned hard sauce is available.

NO-BAKE COOKIES

3 cups quick-cooking rolled oats	1 cup sugar
5 tablespoons cocoa	½ cup milk
½ cup nuts, chopped	½ cup butter
½ cup shredded coconut	

In a bowl combine the oats, cocoa, nuts, and coconut. In a saucepan bring the milk, butter, and sugar to a boil, stirring constantly to combine. Pour mixture over dry ingredients. Mix lightly until blended. Drop by the teaspoonful onto a sheet of waxed paper or aluminum foil. Let stand until firm (about 10 minutes). Yields 4 dozen cookies.

NO-BAKE PUMPKIN PIE

1 envelope plain gelatin	1 teaspoon cinnamon
2 tablespoons water	½ teaspoon ginger
1 cup milk	½ teaspoon nutmeg
1 egg, lightly beaten	1 (14 ounce) can pumpkin

1 ready-made pie crust (prebaked regular or graham cracker)
whipped cream for topping

In a saucepan sprinkle gelatin over water; let stand 1 minute, then stir over low heat until gelatin is dissolved. Blend in the milk, egg, and spices. Continue stirring over low heat until mixture thickens. Blend in pumpkin. Turn into the prepared pie crust; chill until firm. Serve with whipped cream.

GRILLED CHOCOLATE BANANAS

4 bananas
½ cup chocolate chips

Cook over hot coals or in a preheated oven. Do not peel bananas, but cut off the stems. Slice bananas lengthwise in half. Stuff each banana with chocolate chips. Squeeze the banana back together to keep the chips from falling out. Wrap bananas individually in aluminum foil. Place or grill or under the broiler for abut 2-4 minutes each side. Peel and eat.

RICE KRISPIES TREATS

¼ cup butter or margarine
1 package regular marshmallows
or 4 cups miniature marshmallows
4 cup Rice Krispies cereal

In a large pot melt butter. Add marshmallows and stir
until completely melted. Remove from heat and add Rice
Krispies. Stir until well coated. Line a pan with wax paper
coated with nonstick cooking spray. Press mixture. Cool
and cut into squares.

KRISPIES BUTTERSCOTCH-PEANUT TREATS

1 cup butterscotch chips
½ cup peanut butter
3 cups Rice Krispies cereal

In a large pot combine butterscotch chips and peanut butter.
Cook over low heat until smooth. Remove from heat and
stir in cereal until well coated. Line a pan with wax paper,
coated with cooking spray. Chill until firm. Cool and cut
into squares and store in refrigerator.

Snacks

INSTANT HORS D'OEUVRES

Part of the fun of boating and camping is spontaneous entertaining. It's wise to keep on hand a selection of easy-to-assemble hors d'oeuvres for such occasions. Here are some suggestions.

CHEESE AND CRACKERS

TOPPINGS
slices of olives, pickles, baco-bits, cucumber, tomato, sandwich meat, apples, sun-dried tomato, pickle, salami

CONDIMENTS FOR ZIPPY FLAVORS
wasabi	chutney
mango salsa	horseradish
barbecue sauce	hot mustard
mustard/mayonnaise mixture	

CHIPS AND DIPS

Potato and tortilla chips are now conveniently packaged in air-tight canisters that keep the chips remarkably crisp, even after they have been opened.

READY-MADE DIPS
bean dip	avocado dip
salsa	onion dip
chile con queso	hummus

MAKE YOUR OWN DIPS
Avocado:
1 mashed avocado	½ cup mayonnaise
1 teaspoon hot sauce	
salt, pepper, garlic powder to taste	

Onion:
1 cup sour cream mixed with one package onion soup mix.

Mexican:
1 cup sour cream mixed with one package taco seasoning.

PEANUT BUTTER & CRACKERS COMBOS

*Once again peanut butter comes to the rescue. It's an
exceptionally nutritional snack and popular with youngsters.*

Spread a generous layer of peanut butter on a cracker and
top with:

fresh fruit slices (banana, apple, pineapple)
thin slice of sweet onion
miniature marshmallows
jam or jelly
carrot, cucumber, or celery slices
honey

SEAFOOD AND CRACKERS

*Even people who avoid fish seem to enjoy seafood hors
d'oeuvres. Here are some ready-to-serve ideas that go directly
from the can to the cracker.*

sardines (packed in oil or tomato sauce)
kipper snacks
smoked oysters
smoked salmon spread

MISCELLANEOUS JIFFY HORS D'OEUVRES

freshly popped popcorn topped with butter and salt
OR
Italian style popcorn sprinkled with Parmesan cheese
    and garlic powder
marinated artichoke hearts
canned nuts, Chex mix, wasabi dry peas, peanut butter
pretzels
canned shoestring potato sticks

FAST CHEESE FONDUE

1 can Cheddar cheese soup   1 cup grated Swiss cheese
¼ cup white wine   1 clove garlic, crushed
dash of hot sauce

Heat all ingredients in a double boiler (or here's a chance
to use your fondue pot), and stir continually until mixture
is smooth. Serve with French bread that has been cut in
bite-size cubes. Spear the bread and dip into fondue pot,
swirling to coat the bread. Fresh cauliflower or green beans
make excellent dippers, and the calorie conscious will
appreciate this.

Note: The old custom when eating fondue is that anytime a
dipper falls off the fork, everyone must take a sip of wine or
kiss each other. I like both ideas.

FISH BALLS

1 can fish, flaked (any type)   2 tablespoons oil
2 cups mashed potatoes,   salt and pepper to taste
   prepared per package   1 egg
   directions   bread crumbs

Combine fish, mashed potato, oil, and salt and pepper.
Stir in egg and blend well. Shape fish mixture into small
balls, then roll in bread crumbs. Fry in hot oil until golden
brown. Serve with tartar sauce or spicy cocktail sauce.

CHEESE FRITTERS

1 egg, beaten   ½ cup milk
1 teaspoon Worcestershire   ½ onion, chopped
2 cups biscuit mix   1½ cups diced Cheddar cheese

Combine egg, milk, Worcestershire sauce, onion, and cheese; then add biscuit mix and stir until blended. Drop mixture by tablespoons into a skillet with about 1 inch of hot oil and cook for 5 to 7 minutes or until golden brown. Drain on paper towel. Serve with jelly.

DEVILED EGGS

If you suspect friends will be dropping by, keep a supply of hard-cooked eggs handy so you can whip up deviled eggs at a moment's notice.

6 eggs, hard-cooked	1 tablespoon minced onion
1 teaspoon minced dill pickle	½ teaspoon salt
splash of dill pickle liquid	¼ teaspoon pepper
(this is the "secret" ingredient)	⅓ cup mayonnaise (more
1 teaspoon prepared mustard	for a creamier egg)
paprika for garnish	

(double recipe for larger crowd)

Slice hard-boiled egs in half and scoop out yolks. In a bowl, mash yolks with a fork; add other ingredients and stir till smooth. Using a spoon, fill eggwhite shells with yolk mixture. Sprinkle with paprika for color. Arrange on platter and serve.

SPEEDY KEBABS

1 pound Polish sausage, cut in cubes	1 tomato, cut in wedges
1 onion, cut into chunks	1 red or green pepper, cut in cubes

Thread skewer or toothpick with alternating chunks of sausage, onion, tomato wedges, and pepper. Place under the broiler or grill for 5 minutes to heat thoroughly.

QUICK DIP

In a skillet or baking pan, spread 1 large can mild chiles, cover with a layer of mayonnaise, then sprinkle with grated cheese (Cheddar or Monterey or whatever is on hand). Heat until cheese is milted. Serve immediately with crackers or corn chips.

NUTS AND BOLTS SNACK
WHEAT CHEX CEREAL MIX

Make a large batch of this crunchy snack and keep it stored in airtight containers.

6 tablespoons butter	1 cup peanuts
3 to 4 teaspoons Worcestershire	2 cups Corn Chex
1 teaspoon seasoned salt	1 cup thin stick
2 cups Wheat Chex cereal	pretzels

Melt butter in a large, shallow pan over low heat. Stir in the Worcestershire sauce and seasoned salt. Add other ingredients and mix till all pieces are evenly coated. Heat for 45 minutes at 250 degrees, stirring every 15 minutes. Spread on paper towels to cool. Makes 6 cups.

SHRIMP & OLIVE APPETIZER

1 can shrimp, drained	½ cup chopped black olives
1 tablespoon onion, finely chopped	1 tablespoon dry sherry
1 tablespoon vinegar	(optional)
¼ teaspoon pepper	

Blend all ingredients and chill before serving. Serve on crackers.

SARDINE CANAPES

1 can sardines
1 tablespoon lemon juice
1 teaspoon paprika
salt & pepper to taste

½ cup mayonnaise
1 tablespoon capers, drained
dash of soy sauce

Drain and flake sardines. Combine all ingredients. Spread on toast rounds or crackers.

DRIED FRUIT SNACK

A nutritious snack good for any occasion.

dried apricots
dried apples
sunflower seeds
chocolate chips (optional)

raisins
cashew or other nut
other dried fruit (optional)

Mix one cup of each and keep stored in an air-tight container.

GARBANZO SPREAD (HUMMUS)

2 cups garbanzo beans
1 tablespoon garlic powder
OR
3 cloves minced fresh garlic
2 tablespoons chopped parsley

1 teaspoon salt
splash of sesame oil
⅓ cup oil
¼ cup fresh lemon juice

Mash beans with a fork until they become spreadable. Mix in other ingredients. Flavors blend immediately, so this dish can be served without delay. Serve with crackers or pita chips.

HUSH PUPPIES

A traditional early American dish. During hunting expeditions the hounds would yelp at the smell of frying fish. To quiet the animals, hunters would drop bits of cornmeal batter into the fish pan, then throw tidbits to the dogs and shout, "Now hush, puppies."

vegetable oil
1 egg, beaten
¾ cup milk
¼ cup onion, diced

1½ cups cornmeal
½ cup flour
2 teaspoons baking powder
½ teaspoon salt

In a skillet heat 1½ inches of vegetable oil. In a bowl mix egg, milk, and onion. Gradually add cornmeal, flour, baking powder, and salt until well blended. Drop the batter by spoonfuls into hot oil; fry until golden brown on both sides.

CRABMEAT SPECIAL

1 can crabmeat
OR
1 can shrimp, drained
½ teaspoon sherry (optional)

¼ to ½ cup mayonnaise
½ teaspoon lemon juice
¼ cup minced onion
¼ cup minced celery

Mix all ingredients well. Spread on crackers or use as a dip.

SMOKED TURKEY ROLLUP

flour tortillas
1 package cream cheese
1 tablespoon dill

1 pkg. smoked turkey breast
alfalfa sprouts
½ cup avocado slices
   (optional)

Spread cream cheese on the tortilla, sprinkle with dill. Layer turkey, sprouts, and avocado. Roll up and secure with a toothpick. Keep chilled. Slice in pinwheels when ready to serve.

EAST CURRY MIX

3 tablespoons butter
1 teaspoon mustard seed
1 teaspoon (or more)
   curry powder

¼ teaspoon pepper
1 large can potato sticks
1 (6½ ounce) can salted
   peanuts

Melt butter in a large skillet. Add mustard seed, cover, and cook until seeds pop. Add remaining ingredients and stir until heated through.

EGGPLANT DIP

1 large eggplant
1¼ teaspoon lemon juice
½ cup oil

4 cloves garlic, crushed
(or 2 tsp. garlic powder)
salt, pepper, basil to taste

Slice eggplant in half and cook in a pressure cooker for 5 minutes, using the rack and half a cup of water. When eggplant is cool, scoop out the inside. Mash the pulp and add the other ingredients and stir till blended. Garnish with minced basil. Serve with crackers.

CURRIED MEATBALLS

2 cans meatballs in tomato sauce
1 tablespoon curry powder
1 teaspoon garlic powder

Mix all ingredients and heat in a chafing dish or skillet.
Provide toothpicks for spearing the meatballs.

AVOCADO-BEAN DIP

1 can bean dip
½ onion, finely chopped

1 tablespoon mayonnaise
1 can guacamole dip

GARNISH
sliced black olives, chopped tomatoes, shredded cheese

In a bowl, combine bean dip, onion, and mayonnaise. Then
spread mixture on serving platter. On top of bean mixture,
spread a layer of guacamole. Sprinkle garnishes on top.
Serve with corn chips.

SALMON LOG

1 can salmon
8 ounces cream cheese
2 tablespoons horseradish
garlic powder to taste

1 bunch minced parsley
2 teaspoons Dijon mustard
1 cup chopped walnuts

Blend the cream cheese and flaked salmon together. Add
all the ingredients except walnuts and parsley and stir
together. Chill a few hours. Using a piece of waxed paper,
roll the salmon mix into a log. Mix the walnuts and parsley
together and roll the log in this mixture until well coated.
Serve with cracker or bread rounds.

COPYCAT NUT MIXTURE

Make your own blend that tastes like the expensive store-bought mixture.

2 tablespoons vegetable oil
1½ teaspoons salt
¼ teaspoon pepper
½ teaspoon turmeric
1 to 1½ teaspoon garlic powder
2 to 3 tablespoons curry powder

1 cup whole almonds
1 cup blanched hazelnuts
1 cup roasted peanuts
1 cup shelled sunflower seeds
½ cup raisins

In a large skillet heat oil, then add seasonings and stir to blend. Add nuts, sunflower seeds, and raisins, stirring until evenly coated. Cook about 3 minutes, then cool nut mixture on a cookie sheet. Store in an airtight container. Yields about 4½ cups.

MORE CLEAN-UP HINTS

6. To brighten aluminum pots, rub with a small amount of lemon juice, then wash well.

7. Prevent spread of bacteria on the wheel of your can opener by cleaning it with a sponge dipped into a solution of hot water and baking soda.

8. For campers and boaters: keep dishwater clean longer by first wiping off greasy plates with paper towels.

9. For a makeshift dustpan, use a foil pie pan cut in half.

10. To prevent scouring powder from caking, remove from carton and store in a large plasticware shaker bottle.

11. In most cases half a sheet of paper toweling is enough. So get twice as much from one roll by cutting the roll of paper towels in half with a sharp knife —do not slice through the cardboard tube, since that's what makes it fit into a standard-size holder.

(For the entire list of helpful hints, see Appendix, page 142.)

Potpourri

MAPLE SYRUP IN A PINCH

2 cups water
4 cups sugar
½ cup brown sugar

1 teaspoon vanilla extract
1 teaspoon maple extract

In a saucepan combine water and sugars and boil for 10 minutes, stirring to prevent burning. Remove from heat and add the vanilla and maple extracts. Use in place of maple syrup.

MOCK VIENNA CREAM

Use as a topping on desserts.

2 tablespoons margarine
    or butter
1 teaspoon vanilla
8 tablespoons confectioners' sugar
1 tablespoon milk

Beat margarine until fluffy. Add vanilla, sugar, and milk and beat until smooth.

BOUQUET GARNI

1 clove garlic
1 teaspoon dried basil
1 teaspoon dried oregano
6 whole peppercorns

1 tablespoon dried parsley
1 teaspoon dried rosemary
2 bay leaves

Tie ingredients together in a cheesecloth bag. Add bag to stews or soups.

HEARTY HOT CHOCOLATE MIX

Enjoy a rich, satisfying cup of hot chocolate with this do-it-yourself mix.

¾ cup sugar   ½ cup nondairy creamer
⅓ cup cocoa   or powdered milk

Combine ingredients and store in an air-tight container. Add 1 to 2 tablespoons to 1 cup of hot water or milk (regular or low-fat). Garnish with miniature marshmallows.

BUTTERMILK DRESSING MIX

(Tastes like "Hidden Valley")

¼ cup powdered buttermilk   ½ cup cold water
1 cup mayonnaise
½ teaspoon or more of the following spices:
salt   pepper
basil   minced onion
garlic powder   sugar
dry mustard

Blend all ingredients
thoroughly and let stand
at least 1 hour before
serving with a tossed
green salad.

FRENCH DRESSING

1 can tomato soup	1 cup vinegar
⅔ cup salad oil	½ teaspoon paprika
2 tablespoons Worcestershire	1 teaspoon dry mustard
⅓ cup sugar	

1 teaspoon each garlic powder, onion powder, salt

Combine ingredients in a quart jar. Shake well and let sit at least one hour before serving. Delicious on sliced mushrooms or tossed green salad.

ITALIAN DRESSING

Right out of a Sicilian grandmother's kitchen. Now everyone can have Italian dressing as it was intended to taste.

1 cup oil	⅓ cup wine vinegar
1 teaspoon ketchup	½ teaspoon oregano
1 teaspoon garlic powder	salt and pepper to taste
½ teaspoon basil (optional)	dash of Worcestershire
½ teaspoon Italian seasoning	

1 teaspoon minced (dehydrated) onion (optional)

Mix all ingredients in a bowl, dressing bottle, or best of all in a blender, and stir or shake till all ingredients are thoroughly mixed. Use on your favorite green salad or for marinated vegetables.

CAN TO PAN COOKERY

1,000 ISLAND DRESSING

Quicker than you can count to three, 1,000 Island dressing is ready.

1 cup mayonnaise
3 tablespoons pickle relish
⅓ cup chile sauce (or ketchup)
dash of salt, pepper, garlic powder

Blend all ingredients in a bowl. Serve with a crispy green salad.

SPICY TEA MIX

1 (9 ounce) jar orange-flavored breakfast drink powder
¾ cup instant iced tea mix with lemon and sugar
1 teaspoon cinnamon
½ teaspoon ground allspice
¼ teaspoon ground cloves

Combine all ingredients and mix well. Store in an airtight container. For one serving, combine 2 tablespoons mix with one cup boiling water in a cup or mug.

WHOLE WHEAT PANCAKE MIX
HOMEMADE

2 cups whole wheat flour
2 cups unbleached white flour
½ cup yellow cornmeal
⅓ cup sugar

2 tablespoons baking powder
2½ teaspoons salt
½ teaspoon baking soda

Mix all ingredients in a large bowl using a whisk. Store in airtight containers.

TO MAKE PANCAKES USE

2 eggs	1¼ cup milk
2 tablespoons oil or melted butter	1¾ cup pancake mix

BEEF JERKY

1 pound flank or round steak	dash or two liquid smoke
1 teaspoon each:	¼ cup each:
salt, pepper, chili powder, garlic powder, onion powder	Worcestershire sauce, soy sauce, and water

Trim fat from meat. Partially freeze for 1 hour. Slice lengthwise with the grain in ⅛" slices. Combine all other ingredients in a glass dish, then add beef slices (making sure they're covered with liquid) and marinate overnight. Remove slices from marinade and drain. Spread on wire racks placed on baking sheets. With oven door open a crack, bake at 150 degrees for 10 to 12 hours. Store in covered containers.

EASY BEEF SALAMI

5 pounds regular ground beef
¼ cup Morton's "Tender Quick"
   (Do not use any alternate curing salt)
4 tablespoons dry red wine
1 teaspoon liquid smoke
2 teaspoons garlic powder
2 tablespoons chili powder
3 teaspoons pepper flakes, fresh or freeze-dried
1½ teaspoons ground cumin
2 tablespoons brown sugar

In a large bowl mix all ingredients, using both hands. Be careful with the curing salt; make sure it's evenly distributed for an even cure. It's a good idea to sprinkle on a little at a time. Divide meat into four equal portions. Roll each into a log about 6 to 8 inches long with a 2½ to 3-inch diameter. Next, roll each log in a cheesecloth or nylon netting wrapper and tie the ends securely with string.

Place the salami rolls on a platter, cover with aluminum foil, and let them sit in the refrigerator for at least 24 hours, preferably longer, to allow the spices to permeate the meat and for the curing salt to do its job.

Bake salami rolls on a rack for 4 hours in a 225 degree oven. Occasionally roll them back and forth while baking so they don't become flat.

After baking, allow the salamis to cool, then remove netting. Dry the excess grease off with a paper towel. Slice thin and enjoy. The salami will keep for three weeks in the refrigerator and six months in the freezer, but they rarely last that long.

ALL PURPOSE BBQ RUB

2 tablespoons paprika	1 tablespoon cumin
2 tablespoons chili powder	1 tbsp. dry mustard powder
1 teaspoon cayenne powder	1 teaspoon sage & oregano
1 tablespoon garlic powder	⅓ cup salt (or less)
1 tablespoon brown sugar	1 tbsp. ground black pepper

Combine all ingredients. Goes with anything!

CAJUN BBQ RUB

2 tablespoons sweet paprika
1 tablespoon basil
1 teaspoon thyme
1 teaspoon garlic powder

1 teaspoon ground pepper
dash of red pepper
salt to taste
1 teaspoon onion powder

Combine all ingredients. Goes with anything, even popcorn!

SUBSTITUTION CHART

When recipe calls for:	You can Use:
1 tablespoon flour	1 tablespoon arrowroot OR ½ tablespoon cornstarch ¾ tablespoon quick-cooking tapioca
1 tablespoon cornstarch	2 tablespoons flour
1 cup milk (follow directions on package of powdered milk)	½ cup evaporated milk plus ½ cup water OR 1 cup nonfat milk plus 2 tablespoons butter
1 ounce unsweetened chocolate	3 tablespoons cocoa powder plus 1 tablespoon butter
1 teaspoon baking powder	½ teaspoon cream of tartar plus ¼ teaspoon baking soda
½ cup butter (1 stick)	7 tablespoons vegetable shortening
1 cup buttermilk (follow directions on package of powdered buttermilk)	1 tablespoon vinegar or lemon juice plus milk to equal 1 cup
1 clove fresh garlic	⅛ teaspoon garlic powder
1 small onion	1 tablespoon instant minced onion
2 teaspoons minced onion	1 teaspoon onion powder
1 cup dairy sour cream	1 tablespoon vinegar or lemon juice plus milk to equal 1 cup
1 cup heavy cream	½ cup butter and ¾ cup milk
1 cup light cream	⅞ cup milk plus 3 tablespoons butter (for cooking only)

1 cup yogurt	1 cup sour cream
1 cup whipped cream	½ cup nonfat dry milk plus ⅓ cup cold water; beat well, then add a splash of lemon juice, 2 to 4 tablespoons sugar and a dash of vanilla and beat until it peaks.
1½ cups corn syrup	1 cup sugar plus ½ cup water
⅔ cup honey	1 cup sugar plus ⅓ cup water
1 teaspoon dry mustard	1 tablespoon prepared mustard
1 cup tomato juice	½ cup tomato sauce plus ½ cup water
1 cup tomato sauce	½ cup tomato paste mixed with ½ cup water

EQUIVALENCY CHART

When Recipe Calls For:	You Can Use:
4 cups sliced raw potatoes	4 medium whole potatoes
2½ cups sliced carrots	1 pound raw carrots
4 cups shredded cabbage	1 small cabbage
1 teaspoon grated lemon rind	1 medium lemon
2 tablespoons lemon juice	juice from one lemon
4 teaspoons grated orange rind	1 medium orange
4 cups sliced apples	4 medium apples
2 cups shredded cheese	8 ounces of cheese
1 cup bread crumbs	2 slices fresh bread OR ¾ cup cracker crumbs
8 ounces package noodles	5½ cups cooked noodles
1 cup instant rice	2 cups cooked instant rice
1 cup rice	3 cups cooked rice
1 cup macaroni (raw)	2¼ cups cooked macaroni

HOW LONG CANNED FOODS WILL LAST

ITEM	KEEPING TIME IN MONTHS	PACKAGING
almond paste	9	can
apple juice	36	can
applesauce	36	can
apricot	33	can
apricot nectar	24	can
asparagus	36	can
bacon, sliced	18	can
bakery mixes	6	bag or box
baking powder	12	can
baking soda	indefinitely	box
barley, pearl	24	bag or box
beans, dried	12	bag or box
beans, green	36	can
beans, kidney, lima	48	can
beans, wax	36	can
baked beans	36	can
beef, corned	42	can
beef, in gravy	36	can
beets	24	can
berries, black, etc.	22	can
blueberries	18	can
carrots	42	can
carrots	25	jar
catsup	24	bottle
cereal, quick cooking	12	box
cheese, grated	6	container
cheese, processed American	15	can
cherries, maraschino	18	jar
cherries, sweet, dark	24	can
cherries, sweet, light	30	can
chicken	36	can
chili con carne	36	can

chili sauce	24	bottle
chocolate, semisweet cnips	18	package
chocolate, baking unsweetened	24	carton
chocolate syrup	24	can
clams	18	can
cocoa, natural	24	can
coconut, sweetened	18	can
coconut, unsweetened	6	bag
coffee, instant	36	jar
coffee, roasted and ground	12	can
cookies	4	carton
corn, creamed or whole	42	can
corn meal	12	package
crackers, graham	2	box
crackers, soda, oyster	4	box
cranberry sauce	24	can
creamer, nondairy	12	jar
figs	24	can
flavorings: vanilla, maple	indefinitely	bottle
lemon, orange, etc.	18	bottle
flour, rye and wheat	12	bag
frankfurter	48	can
fruitcake	6	box
fruit, candied	6	jar
fruit cocktail	33	can
garlic, dehydrated	24	can
gelatin, plain	36	container
grape juice	18	can
grapefruit sections	30	can
grapefruit juice	36	can
ham	48	can
hominy grits	12	box
honey	24	jar
horseradish, dehydrated	24	bottle
jam or jelly	18	can or jar

luncheon meat	36	can
macaroni	36	box
margarine	24	can
marmalade	18	jar
mayonnaise	6	can or jar
milk, evaporated	12	can
milk, dry	24	box
molasses	18	jar
mustard, prepared	18	jar
mushrooms	30	can
noodles, chow mein	2	can
noodles, egg	24	bag
nuts, shelled, roasted	24	can
nuts, unshelled	6	bag
okra	24	can
olives	24	jar or can
olive oil	6	can
orange juice	36	can
peaches	36	can
peanut butter	36	can or jar
pears	40	can
peas, green & blackeyed	42	can
pickles	18	jar
pie filling, prepared fruit	12	can
pimientos	36	can
pineapple	33	can
pineapple juice	36	can
plums	30	can
popcorn kernels	36	bag
potato chips	2 weeks	package
potato chips	12	canister
potatoes, sweet	30	can
potatoes, white	30	can
prunes, dried	18	can
pumpkin	27	can
raisins, dried	18	can
rice, instant	18	box

rice	24	bag
salad oil (canola)	12	can
salmon	30	can
salt	indefinitely	container
salt, celery, garlic, onion	36	container
sauces: soy, Worcestershire	24	bottle
hot sauce	24	bottle
sauerkraut	18	can
sardines	18	can
shrimp	18	can
syrup	24	bottle
soup, condensed	36	can
spaghetti, any pasta	36	carton
spinach	33	can
starch, corn	36	carton
sugar, brown	18	carton
sugar, confectioners	18	carton
sugar, white refined	indefinitely	bag
tapioca	48	carton
tea	18	can or cart.
tomatoes	30	can
tomato juice	24	can
tomato paste	18	can
tomato puree	30	can
tuna	30	can
vegetable juice	24	can
vinegar	30	bottle
yeast, bakers	1	can

METRIC CONVERSION CHART

LIQUID MEASURES

SPOONS/CUPS	OUNCES	NEAREST EQUIVALENT DECILITERS* & LITERS
1 tablespoon	1 ounce	¼ dL or 1 tablespoon
¼ cup or 4 tablespoons	2 ounces	½ dL or 4 tablespoons
⅓ cup	2⅔ ounces	¾ dL
½ cup	4 ounces	1 dL
⅔ cup	5⅓ ounce	1½ dL
¾ cup	6 ounces	1¾ dL
1 cup	8 ounces	¼ L
2 cups or 1 pint	16 ounces	½ L
4 cups or 1 quart	32 ounces	1L

DRY MEASURES

OUNCES	POUNDS	NEAREST EQUIVALENT IN GRAMS
1 ounce		30 grams
2 ounces		60 grams
3 ounces		85 grams
4 ounces	¼ pound	115 grams
5 ounces		140 grams
6 ounces		180 grams
7 ounces		210 grams
8 ounces	½ pound	225 grams
9 ounces		250 grams
10 ounces		285 grams
11 ounces		325 grams
12 ounces	¾ pound	340 grams
13 ounces		385 grams
14 ounces		400 grams
15 ounces		425 grams
16 ounces	1 pound	450 grams
32 ounces	2 pounds	900 grams
	2½ pounds	1 kilogram

* Deciliter ($\frac{1}{10}$ of a liter)
Centiliter ($\frac{1}{100}$ of a liter)

HELPFUL HINTS

BAKING/COOKING

1. To avoid measuring flour or sugar, pour a premeasured cup into your hand to get an idea of how much fills your cupped hand.
2. For lighter, fluffier pancakes or waffles, use club soda instead of milk.
3. Improvise a colander by punching holes in an aluminum foil pan.
4. Before measuring honey, syrup, or molasses, spray the cup with a nonstick spray.
5. Rather than dirty a bowl for mixing cake batter, use the backpackers' trick and "moosh" all ingredients in a sealed ziploc bag. When ingredients are blended, unzip and pour into a baking pan.
6. Marinate meats in ziploc bags and avoid another clean-up.
7. When dividing a recipe in half, use this rule of thumb for eggs. Lightly beat the egg. 1½ teaspoons equals one-half an egg, 1 teaspoon equals ⅓ egg.
8. Use a strand of uncooked spaghetti to test doneness of a deep cake. (Sometimes toothpicks are too short.)
9. Shape ground beef into patties before freezing. Shape with wet hands for an extra fast and neat job. Separate patties with waxed paper. Frozen patties barbecue just fine.
10. A stale egg will float or tilt to the top of a bowlful of water. Throw out floaters. Fresh eggs should sink to the bottom.
11. For an emergency coffee filter, fit an ordinary, unscented facial tissue into the coffee basket.
12. Avocados will ripen faster in a tightly closed brown paper bag.
13. For delicious flavor, add an orange peel to the teapot a few minutes before serving.

CAN TO PAN COOKERY

14. Use leftover coffee in place of liquid when making tapioca pudding. Add extra sugar and a tablespoon of chocolate syrup to create a mocha flavor.

15. Extend scrambled eggs with that last dab of leftover cottage cheese. (Two tablespoons cottage cheese replaces one egg.)

16. Improvise carbonated drinks by using half a glass of fruit juice and filling the rest with club soda.

17. Use leftover dill pickle juice to marinate carrot sticks: marinate overnight or longer and serve with cocktails.

18. When cooking rice, double the portion and use the cooked rice in meatloaf in place of breadcrumbs, or in cold salads, or make rice pancakes (use one cup rice for one cup flour).

19. An easy way to drain canned food liquid is to first puncture the top and spill off excess liquid before fully opening the container.

20. For short day excursions take along hot dogs in a thermos jug filled with boiling water. Don't forget the buns.

21. Biscuit mix is excellent for breading meats or fish. Use instead of flour or bread crumbs.

22. For variety, make sandwiches using pancakes or waffles (leftover from breakfast) instead of bread. Pita bread, waffles, and tortillas are great too.

23. Add a beaten egg to hot chicken soup for extra nutrition.

24. Don't discard an old fork; bend back the prongs and use to neatly remove pickles from their jars.

25. If you need to soak dried fruit such as prunes or apricots, they'll be more flavorful if soaked in cold tea.

26. No candleholders for a romantic picnic dinner? Core a rosy apple or even an orange and put a candle down the hole.

27. Save time starting a barbecue fire by placing charcoal briquettes into each compartment of a cardboard egg carton. Close the carton and light.

28. When a recipe requires a stove-top casserole be finished in the oven, protect skillet handles from burning by wrapping them in aluminum foil.

29. To liven up canned fruit cocktail, add a shot of rum or brandy an hour before serving. Garnish with miniature marshmallows.

30. Don't forget the "crunch" in menu planning. People psychologically need to get their teeth into something chewy to get that soul-satisfying crunch sound.

CLEAN-UP HINTS

1. Delegate clean-up duties. Immediately write the author if you have a foolproof plan to coerce your crew.

2. Clean and sweeten stainless steel coffee pots and vacuum bottles by placing three tablespoons baking soda into a quart of hot water and letting it stand in the container for 10 minutes. Rinse well.

3. Clean a coffee pot by filling it with soapy water and percolating for 15 minutes.

4. Polish chrome or stainless steel pots with a cloth moistened with white vinegar.

5. To prevent plastic dishware and utensils from becoming stained, add a few drops of bleach into the dishwater. Let heavily stained plasticware soak in a stronger solution for 10 minutes.

6. To brighten aluminum pots, rub with a small amount of lemon juice, then wash well.

7. Prevent spread of bacteria on the wheel of your can opener by cleaning it with a sponge dipped into a solution of hot water and baking soda.

8. For campers and boaters: keep dishwater clean longer by first wiping off greasy plates with paper towels.

9. For a makeshift dustpan, use a foil pie pan cut in half.

10. To prevent scouring powder from caking, remove from

carton and store in a large plasticware shaker bottle.

11. In most cases half a sheet of paper toweling is enough. So get twice as much from one roll by cutting the roll of paper towels in half with a sharp knife —do not slice through the cardboard tube, since that's what makes it fit into a standard-size holder.

Index

Chicken Dishes (Continued)

Tailgate Tortilla 30
Thai Chicken in Green Curry Sauce 64

CLAMS
Artichoke & Clam Casserole 67
Clam & Tuna Chowder 76
Mock Bouillabaisse Soup 45
Quick & Thick Clam Chowder 77
Spaghetti with Clam Sauce 67

COOKIES
Haystacks 107
No-Bake Cookies 112

CORNED BEEF
Corned Beef 'n Cabbage Casserole 56
Mock Reuben Sandwich 35
Hash Burritos 31
Hash 'n Eggs 23

crepes 42

CURRY DISHES
Curried Chicken Pilaf 59
Curried Cream-of-Chicken Soup 75
Curried Meatballs 124
East Curry Mix 123
Indian-Style Chicken Curry 62

D

DESSERTS
Banana Flambé 109
Biscuit Baked Prune 111
Bread Pudding with Fruit 108
Chocolate-Banana Shortcake 110
Chocolate Dessert Fondue 110
Dessert Dumplings 108
Elegant Fruit & Cheese Sampler 109

Desserts (Continued)

DINNER DISHES

Dinner Dishes (Continued)

E

F

G

galley equipment 4

H

I

L

Lunch Dishes (Continued)

M

N

non-electric waffle iron 11

O

P

CAN-TO-PAN COOKERY